Confederate Seas

by

John Peter Hess

ISBN (10) 1-905933-01-0
ISBN (13) 978-1-905933-01-3

Front Cover Image: C.S.S. Alabama.

Designed and typeset by
Heritage Marketing and Publications Ltd
Hill Farm, Great Dunham, Kings Lynn, Norfolk,
PE32 2LP
Tel. 01760 755645
Fax. 01760 755316
e-mail: publishing@heritagemp.com

Heritage
Marketing & Publications Ltd

Contents

Maps and Illustrations

Preface

Confederate Seas was first written in 1955, the research for it being mostly conducted at the Cambridge University Library. The finished book was offered for publication in London then, but was turned down. The reasons for refusal were unstated, but I think they would have been bad English and a lack of primary sources – the book was based entirely on other people's narrative. So matters remained for many years. I had little time after university to do any writing.

In the late 1970s I met Jerry Williams, an enthusiast for the American Civil War, who was kind enough to show me the Liverpool buildings and sites connected with the war. He had produced a small booklet on the subject of Confederate cruisers built in Liverpool, and gave lectures on that subject. However, his work was limited to those ships, and did not cover the wider war at sea. I could see how 'Confederate Seas' might still be worth more of my time, especially if through Jerry I could find some original material about Liverpool. I resolved to look again at it one day – probably when in retirement.

That was the position until last year, when I was indeed retired, and had carried through some other long projected writing. In addition, my work on our family history was complete. I would now try rewriting 'Confederate Seas', improving the juvenile prose and building up the chapter on Liverpool.

The first step was to visit Liverpool Library, to check on publications there. I found immediately that other writers had dealt with the subject I intended, including Liverpool, and that there really was nothing new for me to say. Specifically the books are;

'The British Shipyard Conspiracy in the American Civil War', by D.Hollett, 1993.
'The Rebel Raiders', by J.T.de Kay, 2002.
'The Naval History of the Civil War', by H.P.Nash, 1972.

I have therefore decided to rewrite for my own satisfaction only. One thing I have noticed in the later publications is a change in sentiment over the subject matter. In 1955 writing was sympathetic toward the South, regarding the cruiser captains as gallant warriors fighting in a hostile world, and the South itself as conducting a romantic struggle for freedom. My own writing naturally reflects that attitude. Nowadays the North is seen as the good side and the cruiser captains as pirates. However, I have decided not to change the tone of my book, because that would be false to the original.

Finally, I want to thank Valerie for her essential and excellent job of proof-reading.

John Hess   2005

Introduction

In 1860 the United States was effectively two nations; a South old fashioned enough to be controlled by an aristocracy which approved and made use of slavery; a North full of the new ideas of freedom and enterprise. Those differences and the growing economic dominance of the North had brought the South to the point of withdrawing from the Union of states drawn up as recently as 1776.

It had not been so in the beginning. The original thirteen colonies had come together to gain independence from Britain. All had relied on agriculture, all contained large numbers of small farmers; and from all expansion to the west had taken place. By 1860 there were thirty states, bound originally and in practice by a union of common interest.

In the South the climate and land had favoured the growing of cotton and sugar. Those crops could be best grown on a large scale, so that great estates with relatively few owners had developed. The use of slaves to work them had been learnt from experience in the West Indies, and black slaves were readily available from Africa. In contrast, the northern half of America had a more temperate climate, more suitable to cereals and animals, so that the small farmer pattern was maintained. In addition, great discoveries of coal and iron had been made, and in consequence, manufacturing industry quickly became established. The skills needed in the North had been learnt in Europe, and were those of men of a free and independent disposition.

A steady pressure now built up. Using economic muscle, the north showed its displeasure at Southern slavery, and eventually brought matters to the point when Southern states felt their rights were being violated. Starting with South Carolina in December 1860, those states each seceded from the Union, and formed themselves into a new group, which they called the Confederacy. There would be no reconciliation.

War came in 1861 because the North would not accept a break-up of the United States.

Both sides found themselves able to raise strong and committed armies from the start - there was a fairly even split of officers from the regular army. However, the greater industrial strength of the north meant it could supply itself more easily than the south. Indeed, as time went on the latter turned more and more toward import of armaments and most other manufactured goods. To pay for them, the south had to export their own products, and that meant cotton. It was essential for them to keep their ports and sea lanes open.

Crucially, the United States government managed to hold the loyalty of its navy. At the start of the war, therefore, the Confederacy had virtually no warships to fight the United States or to protect the essential import and export trade. This work is the story of Southern reaction to that situation, and the war at sea which resulted.

A SUMMARY OF THE AMERICAN CIVIL WAR

A list of the most important dates of the war is written below, so that events in the narrative may be compared with the overall military situation.

13th April 1861	First shots fired, leading to capture of Fort Sumter, Charleston, by Confederate forces.
6th May	State of War officially recognised by United States.
21st July	First major battle of war at Bull Run, Virginia. Confederate victory.
16th February 1862	Capture of Fort Donelson by Union forces.
6-7th April	Battle of Shiloh won by Union. Confederate retreat into Mississippi.
28th April	Capture of New Orleans by Union forces.
23rd May-10th June	Shenandoah Valley campaign in Virginia. Confederate victory
26th June-1st July	'Seven Days' battle on Richmond peninsula. Union army assault on Richmond abandoned.
30th August	Second battle of Bull Run. Confederate victory.
3rd-17th September	Invasion of Maryland by Confederates defeated at Antietam.
7th August-8th October	Confederate invasion of Kentucky defeated at Perryville.
23rd September	President Lincoln's proclamation of freedom for all slaves.
13th December	Union advance in Virginia halted at battle of Fredericksburg.
1-4th May 1863	Confederate victory at Chancellorsville, Virginia, but 'Stonewall' Jackson killed.
June-4th July	Confederate invasion of Pennsylvania halted by defeat at Gettysburg.
4th July	Fall of Vicksburg, last Confederate stronghold on the River Mississippi.

10-20th September	Chickamauga campaign in north Georgia. Union retreat into Chattanouga.
23-25th November	Battle of Chattanouga. Decisive Union victory opens way for invasion of Georgia.
March-May 1864	Failure of Red River campaign leaves Texas in Confederate Hands.
May-June	Heavy fighting in Virginia at battles of Wilderness, Spottsylvania, And Cold Harbour. Union attacks defeated with heavy loss.
5th June	Sherman's march into Georgia commences.
18th June	Siege of Richmond and Petersburg by Union forces in Virginia begins.
5th August	Capture of Mobile, Alabama, by Union forces.
27th September	Capture of Atlanta, Georgia, by Union forces, followed by Sherman's unopposed march across south Georgia.
15-16th December	Battle of Nashville. Last attempt by Confederates to win in west fails.
21st December	Capture of Savannah, Georgia, by Union forces.
18th February 1865	Capture of Charleston, South Carolina, by Union forces.
31st March	Defeat of Confederates in Virginia, followed by fall of Petersburg and Richmond.
9th April	Surrender of Lee's Confederate army at Appomattox.
16th April	Assassination of President Lincoln.
26th April and after	Surrender of remaining Confederate forces. Last town to surrender was Galveston, Texas, on 3rd June.

TYPES OF SHIP ENCOUNTERED IN THE WAR – SAIL AND STEAM

Bark or Barque:	Three-masted sailing vessel with fore and main masts square-rigged.
Brig:	Two masted square-rigged sailing vessel.
Clipper:	Sailing ship with forward-raking bows and aft-raking masts.
Coaster:	Any vessel engaged in trade between ports on same coast.
Cutter:	Single masted sailing vessel.
Frigate:	Heavily armed warship, with 20 to 60 guns; may be sailing ship Or steam powered.
Ship;	Any seagoing vessel of considerable size. As sailing vessel, specifically three, four or five square rigged masts.
Schooner:	Fore-and-aft-rigged sailing vessel with two or more masts.
Sloop:	One-masted fore-and-aft-rigged sailing vessel.
Sloop-of-war:	Steamer with heavy armament.
Paddle steamer:	Steam powered vessel with paddle at rear.
Side-wheeler	Steam powered vessel with paddles on both sides.
Steamer:	Steam-powered vessel with rear mounted screw or screws.
Tow-boat or tugboat:	Steam powered vessel designed to move other ships not under power.
Whaler:	Ship designed for whaling.

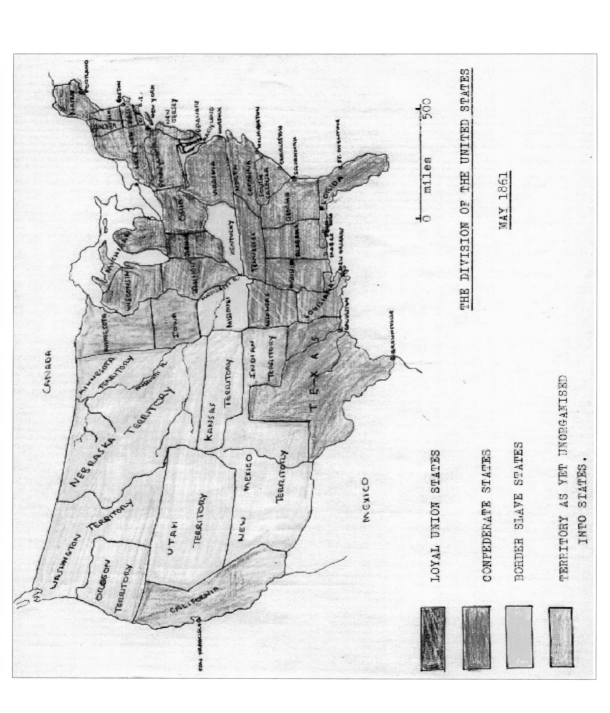

THE DIVISION OF THE UNITED STATES

MAY 1861

LOYAL UNION STATES

CONFEDERATE STATES

BORDER SLAVE STATES

TERRITORY AS YET UNORGANISED
INTO STATES.

CHAPTER ONE

The Privateers

Five days after the surrender of Fort Sumter, President Jefferson Davis of the new Confederacy signed a proclamation to allow 'Letters of Marque' privateers. Such ships and their crews, who in normal times might have been regarded as pirates, gained a legal status in the eyes of their government, and were granted freedom to attack and capture their opponents' merchant shipping.

The Confederates move was certainly prompted by their great inferiority in shipping. Indeed, Davis and Mallory, his secretary for naval affairs, started with virtually no navy at all, and only two naval dockyards - Pensacola in Florida and Norfolk, Virginia, though numerous potential harbours existed around their coast. If the South was to fight at sea, some way of creating a navy had to be found.

Even worse, few merchant ships were owned by southern businessmen, leaving most Southern import and export business to be carried by the United States. That fleet no longer being available, the South looked to neutrals, especially Great Britain, with its demand for cotton, to send in their own shipping. But the United States Navy, armed with the proclamation of a blockade by President Lincoln on 19th April 1861, and facing little opposition at sea, would certainly be able to close off Southern ports, even to neutral ships. How could such a blockade be defeated ?

The 1860s were years of change at sea, when sail was gradually replaced by steam. Thus, around the South and actually available for service was a mixture of the old and new . Nominally the Confederate navy consisted of steamers - the side-wheeler 'Fulton'in Pensacola and the 'Merrimac' at Norfolk, and sailing vessels - six cutters, three coast survey vessels, six lighthouse tenders, and a motley jumble of old river boats. This was poor material with which to fight, although it did include the 'Nashville', whose story will be told later. The Confederates were forced to go into the open market to purchase anything which might float, and by virtue of Mississippi steamboats and the Caribbean trade, established their best fleet at New Orleans. Plans were laid for the building of ironclads, rams and steamers. However, the results were all very inadequate, and few trained sailors were available, anyway.

A better approach was to think about the fleet which had remained loyal to the United States. It was known that over 100 warships were available to them, and that more would, no doubt, be purchased for the blockade of Southern ports. But half of that existing fleet was still powered by sail, and only 42 were genuine steamships. Of the latter, 5 were under repair, others were scattered around the world, and only 12 were immediately ready for blockade duty. In the first few months of the war, before any blockade could be established, the South might effect something at sea, while if the Unites States could in the longer term be forced to divert ships to protect its own merchantmen, there was a chance of rendering the blockade ineffective. Why not try commerce raiding by privateers ?

The international Naval Treaty of Paris, 1856, contained some relevant decisions. This treaty came directly out of the experience in the war of 1812 between Great Britain and the United States. Commerce raiding for profit, or privateering, had reached a menacing level. Now such actions were to be made illegal. Equally, by the treaty, a neutral flag was stated to cover an enemy's goods, except contraband of war, while neutral merchandise, again excepting contraband of war, under the enemy flag, must not be seized. Finally, blockades must only be recognised if effective. Great Britain and many European countries had signed the treaty, would not recognise an ineffective blockade, and would be free to send in ships to bring out cotton. If those were attacked, it would be an act of war, which would suit the South nicely. On the other hand the United States had failed to sign the treaty, and that left the South free in 1861 to appoint its own privateers.

Mallory could see his opportunity. He knew that his privateers would be small ships, incapable of working far away from home. However, he could also see privately owned schooners, cutters and steamboats under the Confederate battle flag cutting off the New England - South American and West Indies coastal trade, and disturbing the large trans-Atlantic trade. With any luck US Navy ships would have to give first priority to guarding their own people.

He therefore announced that the Confederate government would encourage any company or group of men who would fit out a boat of any kind, to operate from any port in the Confederacy to attack, capture and return to Southern prize courts merchant ships of the United States. In case it was necessary, these privateers were guaranteed bounties for ships destroyed, but in general it was expected that prizes would be brought in for adjudication and sale, to the profit of the privateer. One twentieth of that value, however, would go to the government, while the privateers's crew must receive at least 20%. Extra money would be offered to crews able to capture warships. In return, certain rules applied. Privateer owners must apply for a commission or Letter of Marque from the government, and must at the time of application have a suitable craft in possession. Such ships would be inspected before departure to ensure their stated armament and crew were carried. All prizes had to come to government prize courts, while any ship taken inside the three mile limit automatically became the property of the Confederate States without reward. Lastly, to prevent unscrupulous captains preying on neutrals, each was required to keep a journal of his activities for later scrutiny.

What an invitation! Everywhere in southern ports, it seems, the talk turned to profit. Men rushed to combine and find boats. Up north in New England, however, there was a different, if equally frantic reaction. One morning in New Bedford, Massachusetts, frenzied bell-ringing brought the local militia to arms. Two sails had been sighted – surely privateers – and cannon were run out in preparation. Then the sails approached, and the crews of two harmless merchant ships waved happily at such an unexpected welcome.

Soon, however, applications for serious commission were coming in, and just two weeks after the proclamation the 'Phoenix' was prepared and ready at Delaware in Maryland. She was really quite large, being of 1,644 tons, with 7 guns and 240 crew. But Maryland was by April 1861 inclined to favour the Union, and 'Phoenix' never got to sea.

New Orleans was first to produce genuine privateers. Perhaps there was a better chance of finding suitable ships at the mouth of the Mississippi, and, indeed the 'Calhoun' had been a river tugboat, a paddle-wheel steamer of 509 tons. Captained by J.Wilson, and with a crew of 85, she had mounted one eighteen pound gun, two twelve pound and two six pounders. On 16th May 1861 'Calhoun' went down the river, and immediately came across a tempting catch over the bar. This was the bark, 'Ocean Eagle', 300 tons, with a cargo of lime, and flying the United States flag: obviously unaware of the state of war. Fortunately she was still outside the 3 mile limit, and surrendered easily to Wilson. After seeing her up the river with a prize crew, the 'Calhoun' moved out to sea.

On the 18th May Wilson took the steamer 'Milan', 700 tons, carrying salt from Liverpool and bound for New Orleans. It was a rich prize. But before he could turn for home the 'Ella', a small schooner with fruit for Pensacola, was sighted and eventually captured. Wilson came back to New Orleans well satisfied with his first expedition.

After a few days for celebration and repair, Wilson put to sea again, only to be quickly surprised when the privateer 'Ivy', another converted tug, outran him for possession of a prize. There was better luck on the 25th May, when three New England whalers were sighted well out to sea, and soon fell into Wilson's hands, with the oil they were carrying. Up into New Orleans they went as prizes. On the day following that, however, the sudden appearance of U.S.S. 'Brooklyn', a warship of considerable power, caused 'Calhoun' to steam for home. The blockade of New

Orleans now commenced with 'Brooklyn', the first of several warships to arrive. ('Brooklyn' was a steam powered sloop: the others sent initially to cover New Orleans, Mobile and Galveston were 'Powhatan' and 'South Carolina', both steam sloops).

Contemporary with 'Calhoun' were the steamers 'Ivy' and 'Music'. Both owned by the same company, they were locally based ships. 'Ivy' was known as the fastest tugboat on the river, while 'Music' had been a coastal packet steamer. Both were about 200 feet long and about 450 tons, both had been adequately armed with one or two guns, and both were ready and commissioned by 16th May. 'Music' was commanded by T.McLellan, the actual owner, while a Captain Baker was assigned to 'Ivy'.

The two ships went down river together on the 16th, following hard behind 'Calhoun'. 'Music' was immediately successful, catching the 'John H. Jarvis' anchored near the telegraph station at the mouth of the Mississippi. This singularly helpless ship was standing by while her captain walked up to the station to find out what was going on. Now he found himself with a Confederate prize, taken in the name of Jefferson Davis.

The 'Ivy', meanwhile, moved out to sea, and it appears that at 8am the next morning she came into the south-west pass of the river with the steamer 'Marshall'. In taking prizes, the crew of 'Ivy' played the simple trick of pretending still to be a tug, and thus catching Captain Sprague of the 'Marshall' completely unawares.

Another prize that day was 'Abelline', a Boston cargo ship bringing rice to New Orleans, and this turned out to be the only useful capture to McLellan. Both 'John H.Jarvis' and 'Marshall' had been taken inside the three mile limit, and both were forfeit to the Confederate government.

Undaunted, the two privateers set off again, and 'Ivy' beat 'Calhoun', as described above, to their next victim, the 'Sarah E. Pettigrew', another ship carrying salt from Liverpool. After that, a watch was kept at the river mouth for several days, without any ship being sighted. On the 26th May, however, the 'Calhoun' reappeared with fresh prizes, obviously being in a great hurry to get home: what an unpleasant surprise to see the 'Brooklyn' coming up fast behind. 'Ivy' and 'Music' quickly retired up the Mississippi.

The easy days for New Orleans privateers were now over, as a blockade began to form and gradually tighten. Indeed, as news of the war spread, there were fewer targets anyway for the privateers. But much more was to happen on the Delta rivers before the fall of New Orleans in April 1862. When the Confederate cruiser 'Sumter' escaped in June 1861, 'Ivy' was there to help, and that story is told in a later chapter. Another privateer, the schooner 'J.O.Nixon', commissioned in July and captained by Wilson of the 'Calhoun', waited a month at the river mouth for her opportunity. On August 2nd the wind changed in her favour, and she made a dash for the open sea.

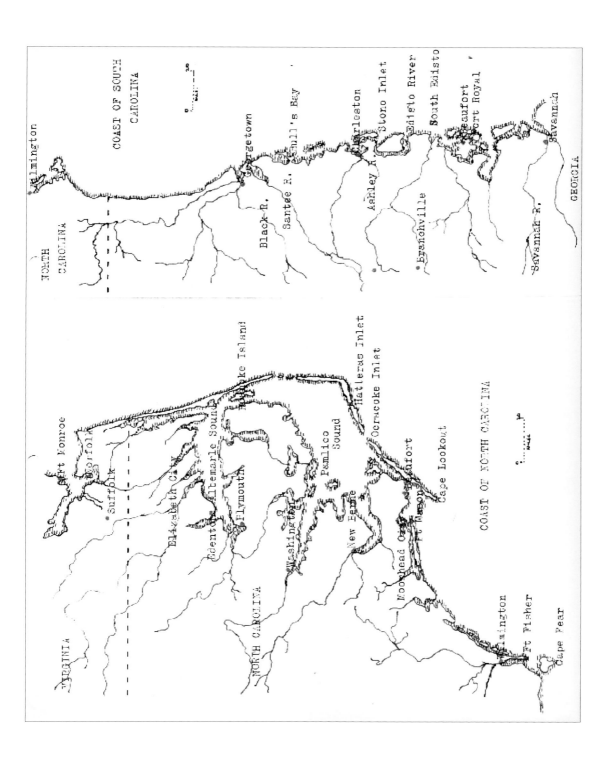

COAST OF SOUTH CAROLINA

NORTH CAROLINA

Wilmington

Georgetown

Black R.

Santee R.

Bull's Bay

Charleston

Ashley R.

Stono Inlet

Edisto River

South Edisto

Beaufort

Port Royal

Branchville

Savannah R.

Savannah

GEORGIA

COAST OF NORTH CAROLINA

VIRGINIA

Ft Monroe

Norfolk

Suffolk

Elizabeth City

Edenton

Albemarle Sound

Roanoke Island

Plymouth

Washington

Pamlico Sound

Hatteras Inlet

Ocracoke Inlet

New Berne

Morehead City

Ft Macon

Beaufort

Cape Lookout

NORTH CAROLINA

Wilmington

Ft Fisher

Cape Fear

'Elsinore' got into Savannah, and helped later, as Union pressure on the city increased, to block the inland channel between it and Charleston.

Several other privateers worked out of Charleston, but didn't quite match those described above. The 'Beauregard' and the 'Petrel', for instance, were caught after mistakenly approaching US navy warships, while 'Lady Davis' took one prize during a short sail, then was converted into a river gunboat. Equally, there was little success for privateers from other ports: the 'Judah', burned during a navy raid into Pensacola, Florida, and the 'Isabel', damaged by blockaders' fire there. The 'Cumberland' sailed from Havana to fit out in a Southern port, but was captured before arrival.

Interestingly, the United States also tried its hand in privateering in this early part of the war. The 'U.S.S. Vanderbilt', later an opponent of the 'Alabama', started life as a privateer, and several merchant ships were armed and commissioned to act as convoy escorts in response to the Confederate threat around the coast. The 'Quaker City' actually took three prizes in a short cruise. However, through lack of further targets, interest was not maintained, and all the steamers concerned were eventually brought into the navy itself, or returned to freighting. After 1861 the United States did not use the privateer.

A slightly different approach was used by the Confederacy along its Atlantic coast. The land for some hundreds of miles is low lying, and there are many inlets, river estuaries and inland waterways. This is especially true of North Carolina, where there is an extra protection for the shore from very long sandbars. Running south from the Virginia state border, such bars enclose about 150 miles of coast, giving rise to the sheltered Albemarle and Pamlico Sounds. One of the most easily passable entrances to the latter is Hatteras Inlet, about 90 miles east of the mainland at New Berne, and because of its easterly situation, quite near the north-south trade route for shipping. On either side of Hatteras the Confederates had erected defenses to protect the inlet, Forts Clark and Hatteras, and supplied them with a few guns. The idea was for armed Confederate gunboats to lurk behind these forts, then pounce out upon passing merchantmen.

To that end North Carolina had gone some way to create its own navy. 'Winslow' was a converted paddle-steamer, 'Raleigh' and 'Beaufort' were river towboats, and these three made up what appears to have been a fairly effective fleet. At any rate, between the 28th May and 11th July they dealt with seven prizes, including some rich cargoes. One was an army transport, moving guns from Key West to the North. Others carried sugar, coffee and salt. Working in this way, only putting to sea when required, the Confederates seemed to hold the advantage: and the blockade, declared some time before, was still too thin.

Eventually, the North Carolina ships were brought into the

Confederate States Navy, as it came to be called, even though their function was retained. In fact they were joined at the Hatteras rendezvous during July by some more privateers, attracted by such good prospects. The ex-pilot boat 'York' came from Norfolk, Virginia, by the Albemarle canal. The 'Mariner', a small steamer, described as being of good speed and armament, sailed north from Wilmington, and the paddle-wheeler 'Gordon' arrived from Charleston.

At once the new ships began to make their presence felt. On the 23rd July 'York' went out to capture a brig, 'B.T.Martin', carrying a sugar mill from Philadelphia to Havana. Equipped with a prize crew, the latter was despatched to Hatteras Inlet, and was only a few miles away from safety when accosted by a Northern warship, the 'Union'. 'B.T.Martin' was chased on to the bar, shelled into submission, and then burned.

On the 25th July both 'Gordon' and 'Mariner' were alerted and claimed one prize each, including the 'William Mcgilvery', a molasses boat, on the Cuba to Boston run. 'Gordon's' captain now took her off on a raid, returning five days later with the schooner 'Protector', another West Indies trader, laden with fruit for Philadelphia.

'Gordon' was again successful on the 4th August, taking 'Henry Butt' and 'Sea Witch', both worthwhile prizes. 'York' was also busy, finding 'G.B.Baker' easy prey, but this time her luck was really out. On the way home, the two ships were met by 'Union', and forced to separate. 'York' ran ashore, could not be refloated, and was burned by her crew; and 'G.B.Baker' was caught by 'Union'.

While all this was going on, loud protests at the trade disruption were being heard in New York, accompanied by claims of ill-treatment of prisoners from escaped merchant sailors. It was plain to the United States that harbours would remain open to the South as long as Pamlico and Albemarle Sounds were in Southern hands. The existing blockade had shown itself ineffective so far – indeed, the distance from Northern ports meant long journeys away from station for their own ships. One solution might be blockships to seal up harbour entrances, but sufficient craft were not available. Instead it had to be conquest.

Once decided, action was swift. By late August an expedition had been gathered, comprising seven warships of variable worth, together with troop transports and a good number of Northern soldiers. On the 20th August 'Winslow' brought in a last prize, the steamer 'Itasca'. On the 27th the Union fleet appeared off Hatteras. As it happened, the 'Gordon' was close by at the time. Her captain realised the game was up, and immediately turned homeward for Charleston.

An interesting and effective combined operation now took place. As the naval ships bombarded Forts Hatteras and Clark, some 320 soldiers were landed on the sand bar. The forts were completely outgunned, and after only a day were obliged to surrender. 600 Confederates became prisoners of war, for the loss by grounding of 'Harriet Lane', a Union gunboat. When a garrison of soldiers, supported by four warships, was left to hold it, Hatteras Inlet was lost to the South, and its continued possession of Pamlico and Albemarle Sounds rendered worthless.

When Port Royal, a fine harbour between Charleston and Savannah, was captured in October 1861, the North obtained their necessary base in the Confederate east, and were thereafter able to dominate the whole Georgia and Carolina coast line. Blockade runners continued to use Charleston, Savannah and Wilmington right through the war, but it became increasingly difficult for them.

It is true to say that coastal privateering in the American Civil War was a short-lived activity. Within a few months nearly all American merchant shipping was keeping away from Confederate shores. Then again, the strength of the blockade and the consequent difficulty in disposing of prizes soon rendered privateering unprofitable. On the other hand, there was still a longer term incentive for the Confederacy to damage United States commerce around the world: and that meant long distance raids with specially designed ships. The procuring of those ships and their subsequent careers make up a large part of the narrative to come in this book.

PRIVATEERS COMMISSIONED BY THE CONFEDERATE STATES IN 1861

Operating from	Type	Tons	Guns	Captain	Commissioned
New Orleans					
'Calhoun'	Paddle steamer	509	5	Wilson	May
'Music'	Coaster	273	2	McLellan	15th May
'Ivy'	Towboat	454		Baker	16th May
'J.O.Nixon'	Schooner			Wilson	3rd July
'Isabella'	Steamer	10			
'Gov. A. Mouton'					November
Charleston					
'Savannah'	Pilot Boat	1		Baker	May
'Jefferson Davis'	Schooner	5		Coxetter	18th June
'Dixie'	Schooner	110	3	Moore	July
'Sallie'	Clipper	170	1	Lebby	October
'Lady Davis'					
'Gordon'	Paddle steamer	519	3	Lockwood	July
'Petrel'	Revenue Cutter	2		Perry	May
'Beauregard'	Schooner	101	1	Hay	
Norfolk					
'York'	Pilot Boat	68	1	Geoffrey	July
Wilmington					
'Mariner'	Steamer		2	Berry	July
Delaware					
'Phoenix'		1644	7		May
Brunswick, Ga.					
'Triton'	Schooner	30	1		April

North Carolina Navy – Hatteras region

Name	Type				Capture by	Date
'Winslow'	Paddle steamer	2		Crossan		May
'Beaufort'	Canal towboat	1		May		
'Raleigh'	Canal towboat	1		May		

PRIZES TAKEN BY PRIVATEERS

Name	Type	Home port	Cargo	Date Taken	Capture by	Sale price or fate
'Ocean Eagle'	Bark	Rockland, Maine	Lime	May 16th	'Calhoun'	$6,800
'Milan'	Ship		Salt	May 18th	"	$9,000
'Ella'	Schooner		Fruit	May 18th	"	
'Panama'	Whaler	New Bedford	Oil	May 24th	"	$1,400
'Mermaid'	Whaler	Providence	Oil	May 24th	"	$8,300
'John Adams'	Whaler	Boston	Oil	May 24th	"	$1,150
'John H. Jarvis'	Ship		Salt	May 16th	'Music'	Confisc. ($14,250)
'Marshall'	Steamer			May 17th	"	Confisc. ($35,000)
'Enoch Train'	Ship		Salt	May 17th	'Ivy'	
'Abelline'	Ship		Rice	May 17th	"	$20,000
'Sarah E. Pettigrew'	Ship		Salt	May 21st		
'Joseph'	Brig		Sugar	June 3rd	'Savannah'	$11,985
'John Welsh'	Brig	Philadelphia	Sugar	July 6th	'Jeff. Davis'	$9,605
'Enchantress'	Schooner	Newport	Glass	July 6th	'Jeff Davis'	(Recapt)
'S. J. Waring'	Schooner	Brookhaven		July 7th	"	"
'Mary Goodall'	Schooner			July 10th	"	Bonded
'M. E. Thompson'		Searsport	Wood	July 10th	"	"
'Alvarado'	Bark	Boston	Wood	July 21st	"	Wrecked
'Windward'	Schooner		Salt	Aug 5th	"	"
'Santa Clara'	Brig			Aug 5th	"	"
'John Carver'				Aug 15th	"	Burned
'Glen'	Bark	Portland	Coal	July 24th	'Dixie'	$3,700
'Mary Alice'	Schooner		Sugar	July 26th	"	(Recapt)
'Rowena'	Bark	Philadelphia	Coffee	July 28th	"	$12,196
'Lydia Frances'	Brig	Bridgeport	Sugar	May	'Winslow'	
'Linwood'	Bark	New York	Coffee	May	"	
'Willet S. Robbins'	Schooner			May	"	
'Transit'	Steamer		Guns	June	"	
'Herbert Manton'	Schooner	Barastable	Sugar	July 3rd	"	
'Hannah Balch'	Brig			June 25th	"	
'B. T. Martin'	Brig	Philadelphia	Sugar	July 23rd	'York'	wrecked
'George Baker'	Schooner			Aug 6th	"	(Recapt)
'Nathaniel Chase'	Schooner			July 25th	'Mariner'	$1,606
'William McGilvery'	Brig	Bangor, Maine	Molasses	July 25th	'Gordon'	
'Protector'	Schooner	Philadelphia	Fruit	July 30th	"	
'Henry Nutt'		Key West	Logwood	Aug 4th	"	
'Sea Witch'	Schooner	New York	Fruit	Aug 5th	"	
'Itasca'	Steamer			Aug 20th	'Winslow'	
'Grenada'	Brig	Portland	Sugar	Oct 12th	'Sallie'	$7,000
'Betsy Ames'	Brig	Wells, Maine	Misc.	Oct 18th	"	$7,000
'B. G. Harris'	Schooner			Oct 29th	"	Released
'Tempest.	Brig			Oct 29th	"	Released
'Elsinore'	Brig	Bangor, Maine	Wood	Oct 30th	"	$8,938
'B. K. Eaton'		Searsport		Oct 30th	"	Burned
'A. B. Thompson'				May 22nd	'Lady Davis'	
'Mary'	Schooner				'Gov. A. Mouton'	

CHAPTER TWO

A Confederate Navy : The Beginning

During the early months of the war, Confederate naval efforts had, by necessity, relied upon private enterprise and activity around the coast. That was never the long term intention, of course, as the South set about creating a force of ships, the Confederate States Navy. However, such a force would inevitably be weaker than the United States Navy, and open warfare on the sea had to be ruled out. Its real purpose would be harrying and destroying the United States Merchant Marine.

Most certainly a target existed. After the Anglo-American War of 1812, the United States had encouraged the building of a merchant fleet and service that set out to rival Britain herself. Through especially the agency and initiative of New England merchants their commerce spread world-wide. Brazilian coffee, West Indian sugar, rubber from the East Indies and rice from China went increasingly via the ships of Maine, New Hampshire and Massachusetts: and soon the resulting prosperity was attracting comment.

A French commentator wrote in 1830; "I cannot help from believing that the Americans will one day become the first maritime power on the Globe".

In 1853 the New York Herald stated; "it must be a matter of sincere satisfaction to every American to know that in both sailing and steam vessels we have surpassed the whole world", while President Buchanan said; "Our commerce now covers every ocean, our mercantile marine is the largest in the world".

Even later, in 1860, Alex. Stevens, vice-president, was able to say; "We have now an amount of shipping which puts us in the front rank of the nations of the world. England can no longer be styled the mistress of the seas. What American is not proud of the fact ?".

Yet there was a weakness, in spite of these years being ones of advantageous transition from sail to steam. The grand old clipper ships, the elegant barks and schooners, and the spry naval frigates, which had all been dominant for so long, were going to be replaced eventually by faster but strange looking paddle wheel and screw steamers, but, of course, there was a reluctance to change among the merchant ship owners: and in 1861 the merchant fleet was still mostly down to sail.

The naval world was also changing. New discoveries were being made in guns and ammunition, which required warships to be altered accordingly – a lower centre of gravity in the water, with armour-plating as a trial option to resist the new guns; the ironclads would soon appear. Many naval ships available in 1861 were still sail powered, but all built in the period around the Civil War had at least to combine sail and steam. If the Confederates could obtain naval vessels of this new type, they would be a serious threat to the older American merchant fleet. For the time being, anything fit for sea and based on steam, must be pressed into service.

The 'Nashville' was a such a steamer, employed before the war in carrying passengers between New York and Charleston. She was a frail ship and even with steam, really too slow for commerce raiding: her side-mounted paddles made her difficult in rough sea. She was, however, the best the rebels managed to seize in Charleston, and was perforce put to use. At first the intention was to run her across to Britain with the Confederate Commissioners, Mason and Slidell (see Chapter 3), but for that purpose she was definitely unsuited. In the end she was given two guns, put under Captain R.P.Pegram, and ordered out to watch the Atlantic routes. While Mason and Slidell went by another vessel, 'Nashville' was supposed to divert the enemy.

Captain Pegram was an ex-US Navy officer, one of few to declare support for the South. His appointment by Richmond confirmed a trust not only in his loyalty, but in the value of his skill and courage, for which he had been prominent in the old navy. Pegram took with him on the voyage Lts. Whittle and Bennett, eleven other officers, including his own son as midshipman, and a crew of sixty.

As darkness came on the night of 26th October 1861 the 'Nashville' was made ready. Making no sound save the churning of her huge paddles, and with no light showing from her black painted sides, she slipped down river. By 11 pm she was clear of Charleston, running near the lea shore towards the outer bar and the blockading fleet. The night was comfortingly dark, overcast, hiding her creamy wake, but as she approached that barrier near midnight, clear sky began to push in, exposing her to possible view from the U.S.S. 'Tuscarora' and one other gunboat, about four miles across the water. Fortunately they failed to spot her against the darkened land, and soon 'Nashville' was out and away.

One disadvantage of any ship relying entirely on steam was the constant need to top up its coal bunkers. 'Nashville' had begun her journey with fairly low stocks – the Confederacy was short of coal, just as everything else – and so her logical first call was to the coaling station on Bermuda : arriving to a grand reception three and a half days out of Charleston.

Bermuda was then a British colony, and should certainly have respected the international rules of neutrality. By the rules no ship of a warring nation should receive more coal from a neutral than was necessary to carry her to the nearest home port. This restriction was also intended to apply to repairs, and naturally to other provisioning. 'Nashville', the first Confederate ship to reach Bermuda, received 600 tons of coal, a very liberal supply, and much more than needed for a return to Charleston. Was this pro-Southern prejudice on the part of the British ? It definitely was, and contrasted with their strictly neutral behaviour towards ships of the United States. In fact, such bias would eventually be found in most British colonial ports, and caused quite a deal of resentment among Americans. Bermuda itself remained a haven for Southern blockade runners right through the war.

Actually, 'Nashville' had been lucky to get into Bermuda at all. A hunt for the raider was already under way, and just a day before her arrival, the U.S.S. 'Connecticut' had passed by to investigate.

Never mind ! Part of 'Nashville's task was, as described, to attract attention to herself and away from the Mason and Slidell expedition. Accordingly she left Bermuda on 5th November, and struggled eastwards into increasingly heavy weather. It was slow going, but, on the 19th, during a quiet interlude in the storm, and only 40 miles from Ireland, she came across the New York steamer 'Harvey Birch'.

From the captain's point of view, there was no sense in taking on an armed cruiser, so down came her colours and 'Harvey Birch' was surrendered. Her crew made their way over to 'Nashville', finding themselves locked up below – only the three senior officers and a passenger were allowed to stay in acceptable surroundings. Some movable and useful property followed, but then the captive freighter was put to the torch. She had no worthwhile cargo to take away.

An interesting document occasioned by this action has survived, a statement signed by the prisoners, as follows;

"We, the undersigned officers and passenger on board the United States Ship 'Harvey Birch' – now being prisoners on board the Confederate States Ship 'Nashville', do pledge to our own captain our sacred honour not to bear arms against, or in any manner to countenance hostilities against such Confederate States until our regular exchange or discharge.

Sgnd. W.H.Nelson, Master   F.Stewart, Second Mate
        C.F.Stevens, Mate   T.Lofbys, Boatswain

> J.Blydenburgh, Passenger
> P.Hallett, Carpenter"

The remainder of the crew were placed in irons until the 'Nashville' reached Southampton, but this was in no way standard practice on Confederate ships. In fact, the usual procedure was to allow parole after a document such as the above had been signed.

'Nashville' continued her journey. Being short of fuel again, she went straight to a 'friendly' port, arriving in Southampton on the 21st November, and for the first time a Confederate flag appeared in British waters. Re-coaling began immediately, and opportunity was also taken to place her in dry-dock for re-caulking.

Once again, however, the neutrality laws were to be tested. On December 15th the U.S.S. 'Tuscarora' arrived off Southampton, having followed 'Nashville' across the Atlantic, and at once a cat and mouse game began. By the rules as they stood, the Confederate ship was supposed to leave harbour as soon as necessary repairs were complete, while her enemy had to wait, and could not attack within the port. On the other hand, if one of the ships left, the other must wait 24 hours before pursuing. Here was a problem for the senior British naval officer in Southampton, Captain Patey, who had the task of seeing that laws were respected, and yet had to urge 'Nashville 'to leave. Repairs could be strung out – indeed, Captain Pegram complained of American spies holding up his efforts to be ready - while Patey would have to explain daily to the American ambassador why he was still allowing the Confederate to remain. Then again, the 'Tuscarora' was kept in steam, and her Captain Craven seemed to behave always in a threatening manner. Eventually, a British warship was sent out to act as buffer between the two, so close to fighting did they seem.

December passed and January wore on. On the 13th 'Tuscarora' left her anchorage, passed the Calshot lightship, but returned in the evening. Twice more she repeated this strange manoevre, on the 15th and 20th, apparently trying to tempt Captain Pegram out – unsuccessfully, as it happened.

By the 25th January Nashville was declared ready to leave, but still she could not, because the United States ship was blocking the way. Captain Patey negotiated, received promises from both parties to observe the 24 hour rule, and was finally told by his own government to send 'Nashville' away on the 28th , only allowing 'Tuscarora' to leave on the 29th. Then Captain Craven sent word that he was leaving on the 28th, and, in fact, did so, only to appear again later the same day, complaining of bad weather. The British were obviously annoyed by this little bit of bad faith, said so, and told Captain Pegram of 'Nashville' not to leave until matters were under control. In the end, the Americans finally agreed not to interfere, and 'Nashville' was able to leave calmly on 5th February, while 'Tuscarora' lay at the coaling berth.

After a 16 day cruise through stormy weather, 'Nashville' made landfall once again in St. George's Harbour, Bermuda, having sighted no enemy at all during her crossing, but now carrying a disabled engine, and suffering much from wear and tear. With only one victory to her credit, too, 'Nashville' may have seemed a disappointingly unsuccessful commerce raider. Her captain resolved to run for home.

On that voyage, however, came some compensation, because on the 26th February she came across the American schooner 'Robert Gilfillan', with a cargo of foodstuffs. That cargo being transferred to 'Nashville', the schooner was sunk by burning.

Approaching the Confederacy in February 1862 was a very different matter from when she left in October 1861. Much had happened in a few months, and many more enemy warships were patrolling the coast. Port Royal had fallen in November, giving the United States a local harbour, Savannah was almost completely closed, while the whole Hatteras area was unavailable. Even Charleston was getting more difficult for any ship but a specialist blockade runner. The options for 'Nashville' now were limited, and when Captain Pegram found himself off the less important town of Beaufort, North Carolina, where only one enemy warship could be seen, he resolved to try for it. Pegram hoisted a United States navy flag, and steamed directly toward the blockade vessel, 'Albatross'. This had to be dangerous, because the latter definitely outgunned the 'Nashville'. Steadily the ships closed, until only musket range apart. Then suddenly up went the Confederate flag, as 'Nashville' swept by to safety. Wild shooting from 'Albatross' accomplished nothing, and the journey was over. 'Nashville' soon lay snugly below the guns of Fort Macon.

It was never true to say that her cruise had been a failure. 'Nashville's role as a diversion had been important, and numerous United States warships had been evaded, in spite of $200,000 reward offered for her capture. 'Nashville' had made a positive contribution.

Sensational though her escapes had been, and however much trouble 'Nashville had caused, she was now considered too slow for a successful commerce raider – only two ships seized. Captain Pegram reported as much, and she was never used again for the purpose. As the war continued, and with Beaufort being captured in April 1862, 'Nashville' was driven through the blockade to become part of Savannah's local defense. She was left in that role until February 1863, when the U.S. monitor 'Montauk' caught her stuck on a sand bar, and shelled her to destruction.

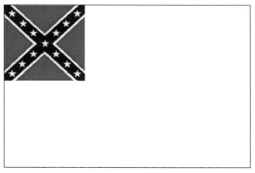

Second Confederate Naval Ensign, 1863: the 'Stars and Bars'. A later ensign had a red band running along the outside edge of the flag.

The first Confederate Naval Ensign, 1861: seven stars representing the original seven states of the Confederacy.

CHAPTER THREE

Cruise of the Sumter

At the outset of the Civil War a number of United States naval officers handed in their commissions and declared themselves for the South. Foremost among these was Raphael Semmes, a middle-aged man from Alabama, who, in addition to being a fine sailor, was a qualified lawyer and had worked on the Lighthouse Board in Washington. The hard lines on Semmes' face showed a stern, if not stubborn disposition, but twinkling, merry eyes were an indication of his sense of fun. He was a quiet and religious man, of studious habits, very thoughtful, but ruthless in execution of what he considered right. No man for foolish risks, this Semmes, but even so flexible in mind; above all his virtues shone an undying love of the South and a fierce determination to put her case before the world. He was an ideal captain for a commerce raider, strong, a leader of men, with a fair share of common sense, and with a knowledge of naval law that would stand him in good stead. On the oceans there are no courts, no higher authorities to direct a decision. He alone might provoke a war, but not if he knew the right thing to say or do.

When Jefferson Davis met this man he knew that Semmes was the one he wanted. The first problem of the Confederate Navy was to get ships to sea. In accordance with their policy they had seized the merchant screw steamer 'Savannah', lying in harbour at New Orleans, and had renamed her 'Sumter', in honour of the first action of the war. There was the ship, now the man. When Semmes came knocking at the door, applying for a command, he was a godsend to the Confederate Navy. Thus, on April 18th 1861, Captain Semmes was ordered to join his new ship, the C.S.S. 'Sumter', in New Orleans.

However pleased Semmes must have been with his appointment, he could only have felt some disillusionment in seeing his 'Sumter', a barque rigged steamer. The ship was by no means ready for sea, nor could it yet be described as a warship. As Semmes stood on the deck for the first time, his chief lieutenant beside him, he would have noticed the high lines and solid build of the steamer, whose auxiliary masts were hardly correct in height or distance apart for its size. Too little sail could be hoisted. This ship would break no speed records. There was much to do. The 'Sumter' needed an overhaul, those deck cabins must be removed to give her a lower silhouette and greater buoyancy. The deck itself must be strengthened for carrying heavy guns, while three lifeboats at least must be shipped for safety. More coal bunkers, suitable for long periods at sea, were needed; magazine, shell room, water tanks and one hundred other things were missing. Semmes could guess that his initial resolve to leave port before the blockade formed was going to be unrealistic.

New Orleans was not a naval base. It had been fitted for light repairs only; there was no dockyard, nor any man versed in naval engineering. Everything would have to be improvised, and all work carried out by civilians. He and his officers would have to supervise the labour, while all necessary materials would have to be fetched from other parts of the Confederacy: in time of war, a formidable task.

From the first day Semmes and his 'Sumter' were a centre of activity in the town. There was great enthusiasm for privateering, promoted by the government's proclamation in favour, and already in April, as described in a previous chapter, privateers were fitting out. Yet the busy dockyard hum and clatter around 'Sumter' soon became conspicuous, with eager volunteers swarming over her by the hundred. Problems were solved every day by enthusiastic invention and initiative, and if will alone could have done the trick, she would have been ready to leave within the week. That was too much to hope, of course, when supplies were not to hand and inadequate machines broke down.

Then there was a fear of accidents, caused by the very rush. Amateurish apparatus is notably unstable, and, although no lives were lost by the work, stoppages did occur frequently. In fact, the only fatality was the drowning of Midshipman Holden, when carrying out an anchor in a small boat.

Delays in transport piled up. The water tanks were weeks late. Semmes had ordered his artillery from Norfolk Navy Yard, where much captured material was stored. However, Norfolk was in Virginia, at the other end of the Confederacy, and everything had to pass over miles of overcrowded railway. When the train got lost, Semmes had to send one of his officers, Lieutenant Chapman, in search.

That was the situation on May 26th, when the privateer 'Calhoun' came back to New Orleans with the news of the Mississippi blockade. 'Sumter' no longer had an opportunity to avoid it, and would eventually have to slip past.

The guns did turn up in the end. One had been found, apparently, lying on its side in a wayside station, tipped off and abandoned, while the freightcar had been commandeered by the army. 'Sumter' would have four 24 lb howitzers of 13 cwt each for the foredeck, and an 8 inch shell gun, a weapon designed to pivot about the central deck, where it could be used for warning shots and signals.

The final preparations were made, ammunition came down by boat from Baton Rouge, and the 'Sumter' was commissioned with ceremony and celebration on the 5th of June. Her Confederate Naval flag flew high, a present from the ladies of New Orleans. 'Sumter' was ready to leave her berth: first for trials down river, then to sea.

Raphael Semmes had gathered around him an effective group of officers. Of the senior officers, his First Lieutenant, Kell, was an old friend from the US Navy, who Semmes had asked for directly. Kell was a calm, intelligent man, with a smooth but affable manner. Their acquaintanceship sprang from years before, when Kell, a proud man decended from an old Georgia family, serving as a midshipman, had refused a menial task aboard his ship. Only Semmes' agile brain and swift defence at the court-martial had saved the younger man. Now Kell was middle-aged, a wiser person, and devoted to his protector.

Much of the wardroom conversation would be dominated by the lively second officer, Chapman. He was a youngish man, dark in looks with a bushy beard, but possessed of a clever wit. However, Chapman was considered a capable and resourceful officer, well able to hold his own at sea. He came from Alabama.

In contrast, the third officer, Stribling, was a tough, determined character, whose slow South Carolina drawl might give a false impression.

The fourth officer was William Evans, a young man of 24 years, slim and delicate looking, pleasant in conversation and devoted to the South. Evans could argue anyone into the ground on naval topics, because he had studied at the Naval Academy before resigning to join the Confederates.

Other officers now aboard were Francis Galt, surgeon and ex naval doctor, from Virginia; Henry Myers, paymaster, a South Carolinian; Miles Freeman, chief engineer; B.Howell, Lt. of Marines, brother-in-law of Jefferson Davis himself; and Midshipmen Hudgins, Hicks, Armstrong and Wilson. Other engineers were Brookes, O'Brien and Cummings.

There had been no lack of seamen to fill the crew. Patriotic fervour was reaching a peak in New Orleans, and men were eager to press forward into service. In spite of that, the majority of experienced sailors were foreigners whose ships had been left stranded by the war, and who looked for reward from a commerce raiding voyage. There were 77 sailors and 12 marines.

With this full crew and his choice of officers, Semmes must have felt some optimism about the conflict to come, even though he knew

'Sumter' to be rather makeshift and slow. If only they could avoid direct confrontation with any of the newly built and fast United States warships, all might be well, and they might inflict a lot of damage on the American merchant fleet. Time would tell.

After her trials 'Sumter' dropped down river, cruising easily with the current, and anchored at the head of passes to await her chance. There were numerous channels for escape, of course, but by now all were covered by blockading warships – so the eyes of Captain Semmes were provided for her by the privateer 'Ivy', which sailed up and down to spy out the chances. Suddenly 'Ivy' rushed up to urge Semmes on; the 'Powhatten', a warship much too strong for 'Sumter' to face in battle, and which normally lay beyond the outer bar of the south-western channel, had disappeared. Semmes signalled quickly for a pilot, but reactions on shore were slow; before he could move, 'Powhatten' was back in place.

For eight more days the cruiser lay waiting. Visits from New Orleans were frequent, while Semmes had more coal sent down to him. In the meantime, a tightened crew discipline was created, with cleaning ship becoming a daily routine. There was always to be an officer of the watch on duty, even in port, and uniform had to be worn at all times. Anyone on shore leave had to be back by 10 pm. Gun handling exercises were frequently carried through, while the marines had their own drill to perform. 'Sumter' came up to scratch as a ship of war.

On the 30th June 'Sumter' was lying quietly between the thickly wooded banks in the delta, when 'Ivy' appeared again in a tremendous hurry. The U.S.S 'Brooklyn' had gone from Pass a l'Outre, off to chase a sail just sighted.

Now 'Sumter' could go, pilot or not, and down river the old ship swept, timbers shuddering at the exaggerated speed; down through the Pass a l'Outre and almost out into open sea. There, to their surprise and horror, was 'Brooklyn', coming back, racing on a converging course towards the narrow entrance of the pass, and with her sails fully set going faster than 'Sumter' ever could. Fortunately, 'Sumter' had a head start to reach the pass entrance, and as she left it behind, made a sharp turn to starboard to run from 'Brooklyn'. A rain squall hid them for a few minutes, but it was obvious that the Union vessel was catching up quickly. All seemed lost. Then Semmes had an inspiration. He turned his ship upwind, so 'Brooklyn' had to follow. In the chase neither vessel could now make headway by sail, and using steam alone 'Sumter' was at least equal to her task, in fact surprisingly faster. 'Brooklyn' soon dropped away astern, and was eventually observed to give up the pursuit and turn again for Pass a l'Outre .

Semmes' intention was to cruise south-east until he reached the vicinity of Cuba, where he might hope to disrupt the American sugar trade. From there he planned to move on to Barbados – a friendly British port, please note – where he could refuel and strike south along the Brazilian coast. The South American routes were busiest of all. After that, events would determine his course.

All through the 1st of July 'Sumter' steamed across a south-westerly breeze, through otherwise glorious weather. Her bows rose gently against the light swell, with a slight corkscrew motion unnoticed by her sea-hardened crew. Aboard, the watch had eyes open for their first sail, but nothing happened all day. The marines drilled and Semmes waited. On the second day, Cape Antonio, the western tip of Cuba, was sighted, and, as the wind changed, 'Sumter' used sail alone to turn along the southern coast. Still, patience was in order….and was rewarded.

Right against the low cliffs stood out a sail inshore, beating windward. She was flying the United States flag, and blissfully unaware of her enemy – and why should there be anything to worry about. 'Sumter' at this stage flew a British ensign. Until she was one mile away Semmes kept up his pretence, then hoisted the Confederate flag. A shot across her bows brought the 'Golden Rocket' to a standstill. A Confederate ship in these parts ! It was unbelievable.

The 'Golden Rocket' came from Maine, and normally carried sugar. Just now, however, she had no cargo, being in ballast, and Semmes decided not to waste any time, but to burn the prize at once. This being accomplished, 'Sumter' continued on her way, with prisoners accommodated down below.

On the 4th of July they struck again, this time near the approach to Cienfuegos, and four sugar brigantines were taken. The 'Cuba' and 'Machias' were at first taken in tow, but when 'Cuba' broke her line, she was given a prize crew, and told to follow the others towards port. Just as 'Sumter' reached the entrance, however, she encountered 'Ben Dunning' and 'Albert Adams' coming out. Both fell to the Confederate.

'Sumter' and her four prizes remained at the entrance overnight, and, believe it or not, three more sugar traders came out in the early morning. All were captured. Less satisfactorily, the 'Cuba' had vanished, and never did come back. She had, in fact, been retaken by her crew. When Midshipman Hudgins, in charge of 'Cuba', climbed the rigging to get a better view, his prize crew turned traitor, released the original and imprisoned sailors, and held Hudgins up the mast, while they turned for home.

Meanwhile, Semmes headed for Cienfuegos harbour, escorting his six remaining prizes. Shots were fired over 'Sumter' at this point, bringing the Confederate to a halt. Lt. Evans went ashore to find out how things stood, only to be told it was a matter of establishing nationality of the raider. Once that was cleared up, the facilities of the port were generously offered by the Cubans. However, being still uncertain of the part this

strange ship was playing, they insisted that the six prizes should be held
under guard until their governor gave permission to release them.

This did not please Captain Semmes at all. He couldn't wait until
courts decided their fate. He wrote immediately from 'Sumter' to the
Spanish governor, explaining his position, and employing for the first
time on the voyage his excellent knowledge of maritime law. Meanwhile
Chapman had gone into Cienfuegos to arrange for refuelling, and there
he was approached by two locals with, as they put it, great feeling for
the Southern cause. Could they not help in the disposal of the prizes ?
Now this was just what the Confederates were looking for, and Semmes
quickly appointed the men his agents for the six. 'Cuba' he gave up for
lost, as was indeed the case.

After taking on 100 tons of coal and 5,000 gallons of water, Semmes
put to sea again, his next objective the Cayman Islands. Passing those
lonely rocks with one sighting only, and that a Spaniard, 'Sumter' was
off Jamaica by the 9th of July, plunging headfirst into an easterly gale. It
was hard work for the steamer, and a speed of only five knots could be
sustained. By the 13th the wind was blowing wildly, and all progress had
ceased, while coal was disappearing fast. So bad had been the motion that
Semmes himself had been thrown down stairs, and had to rest in bed for
a day. Nothing for it, in fact, but to give up the Barbados project, and
turn south with the wind; sail alone would carry them away from those
storms. That did the trick. The 15th of July saw them cruising rapidly but
easily in a fresh breeze right up to the Dutch island of Curacao.

At 4 pm they came to St. Annes, an old harbour on the north coast, and
Semmes let off one cannon shot to announce their arrival. This brought
a response eventually in the form of a small sailing boat, which came
quickly alongside. A message was passed up, saying that the governor
refused entry to the Confederates. Hardly a cordial welcome, but such
tricky situations were made for 'Sumter's crew. In this case the trouble
was, no doubt, the presence of a United States consul, who would be
bringing diplomatic pressure to bear. Semmes decided on a personal
approach, sending Lt. Chapman into St. Annes to negotiate. Within a
few hours the governor had changed his mind and 'Sumter' eased into
the port, still flying her battle flag. It seems the consul had employed
threats in his arguments, and that had worked against him.

At once the silence of the outer waters was dispelled as 'Sumter' was
surrounded by small boats, 'bum boats', full of locals selling monkeys,
fruit and bright clothing. Excitement was intense. The first thing the
sailors noticed on their shore leave was a large American flag above a
doorway, which turned out to be the entrance to a hotel. Its proud owner
had hung out his banner in defiance of the governor's recognition of
'Sumter's crew as friends.

One interesting happening at St. Annes was the affair of the South American revolutionary Don Castro. This enterprising man approached Captain Semmes, and requested transport for himself and twenty men to Venezuela, not far away. He even suggested the Confederates might like to join the revolution, which he was about to incite, by becoming their naval force. Semmes was polite in refusing.

After painting ship, coaling and reprovisioning, all paid for with good Confederate money, and everything being ready by the 24th of July, 'Sumter' set off again to a tumultuous farewell from the people of St. Annes. They had been generous indeed in their hospitality. By now, however, Semmes had decided to sail down the South American coast, on the look out for American shipping.

The 25th dawned bright and hot, and, sure enough, there was a sail on the horizon. All day 'Sumter' steamed after that sail, towards evening finally catching up with 'Abby Bradford', a schooner out of New York. She was carrying provisions for Puerto Cabello, and, as such, was a worthwhile prize. Semmes despatched her with a prize crew to New Orleans. This chase had carried 'Sumter' well south along the Venezuelan coast, almost to Puerto Cabello itself, and by the next morning she was able to enter harbour without the help of a pilot.

Puerto Cabello was a very quiet place. Its crumbling ruin of a fort offered only a little protection against anyone wishing to attack it. Awake, it did, though, as 'Sumter' arrived, with all the promise of business at hand. Much less pleased, however, was the governor, who knew what the 'Sumter' represented, and who was obviously mindful of his small amount of trade with the United States – a lifeline for the port, which functioned through vessels like the 'Abby Bradford'. He ordered Semmes to leave.

Now Semmes had no desire to provoke an international incident; after all, he might need the South American ports in time of crisis. Wisely, he decided to back down. But, as they steamed out to sea, the barque 'Joseph Maxwell' was sighted, as it turned out, another of the few United States trading ships in those waters. Having taken possession, Semmes sent word into Puerto Cabello that he would sell the neutral cargo to its Venezuelan owners. Again the governor struck back. His reply was to say 'Joseph Maxwell' had been captured illegally inside the territorial waters of Venezuela, and must be returned at once. Semmes refused these terms. Instead he sent all the prisoners ashore, then placed a prize crew on 'Joseph Maxwell' to sail her to Cienfuegos. There she was to join the group being dealt with by those fresh Confederate agents.

From the coast 'Sumter' now pushed east, passing Tortuga on the 28th of July. Two days went by, in which she steamed through very calm seas under a heavy blanket of fog. Soon Port of Spain, Trinidad, was near; and once again her approach seemed to create a cause for celebration. 'Sumter' already had a reputation, and as usual at a British port was admired and feted. An outgoing British warship even saluted her Confederate colours, a new experience for Semmes and his crew. After identification had been established by friendly officials, permission was given for full coaling and provisioning facility for the visitors. The British attitude was in sharp contrast to that of other neutrals.

Here is just a small story to show how this British behaviour could distort the situation. In port at Trinidad at the time, and ready to leave, was a Maryland ship. The captain, fearing for his ship, came meekly over to ask permission to go without molestation, and this freedom was promptly granted by Semmes – in a British port. It was certainly not in Semmes' interest to sink ships from a state which might still join the Confederacy. Nevertheless, the point was made. With the help of Britain a Southern Confederate might dominate the sea lanes.

While 'Sumter' was in Port of Spain, news came that the six prizes at Cienfuegos were to be handed back to their original owners. Pressure from the United States had been effective (see note 1). Semmes made the decision not to send prizes into neutral ports in future, but rather to burn them if despatch to a Southern port was impractical.

Leaving Trinidad by the way she had come, 'Sumter' passed between that island and Tobago on August 5th, and cruised south along the South American coast. The rain had ceased, to be replaced by sunny, quiet weather, but no other ships were sighted – their only company alongside being flying fish. Soon they were near British Guiana, hoping to reach Maranham, Brazil, 550 miles away, within a few days, but were also running short of coal again. Next they tried Cayenne, but, being rejected there, Semmes opted for Paramaraibo, Dutch Guiana. All at once a sail was seen; it looked very like a warship, perhaps American, but after some minutes of tension, was identified as being French. Semmes hoisted a French flag. The two exchanged courtesies, and both went into Paramaraibo.

More trouble awaited 'Sumter' in port, because again a United States consul was present, determined to stop their recoaling. At one stage 40 tons of coal were tipped into the harbour by his efforts. Here also the news was worrying, with reports of a Northern warship arriving at Trinidad looking for 'Sumter', and others not far behind. Semmes decided to move on. Coaling finally complete on the 31st of August, he sailed north for eight miles, trying to give a false impression to those watching. Then he headed south-east, and by the 4th of September passed through red and muddy water marking the outflow of the Amazon. Entirely under sail they made good progress, in one day alone travelling 175 miles.

One sail was sighted, but, being too far away on a diverging course, was ignored. So far these waters had proved fairly barren for the Confederates, and given that most of his previous captures had been returned to their owners, Semmes was anxious to find something American. On the evening of the 5th of September the weather began to deteriorate, with all the signs of an approaching storm, and although he was near the coast and not far from Maranham, Semmes put down a sea anchor to ride out the rising waves and gale. With a sharp crack the anchor cable snapped, and the ship ran free. 'Sumter' struggled, then crunched into an uncharted sand bar. That was dangerous, but the very next wave lifted her over and into calm water. Next day a pilot arrived from Maranham and the crisis was over.

Maranham (later renamed Sao Luis) seemed hospitable – the Confederates were popular. There was a festival going on, and the battered 'Sumter' added a new dimension to the celebrations. Brazilian sailors were full of praise for them, and even when an attempt was made by the authorities to isolate her crew, pushed by another American consul, Semmes managed to overcome it all. 'Sumter' refuelled at leisure.

Hoping to hear news from home, Semmes lingered in Maranham for several days. However, rumours of United States warships coming soon unsettled them all – a gunboat was said to be just outside the harbour. Semmes paid his bills, and on the 15th of September sailed anxiously out of Maranham. No gunboat was seen.

The cruiser stood north-east. On the 25th their long wait was rewarded at last, as the brigantine 'Joseph Parke' sailed happily, across their path, seeing only a United States flag on the 'Sumter'. When their Confederate colours appeared, and a shot had been fired, she surrendered quickly.

'Joseph Parke' was only carrying ballast, and probably the most valuable gain from her was knowledge of the battle of Bull Run in Virginia. Victory had gone to the Confederates, it seemed, and the fall of Washington was expected daily. Cause for celebration, indeed ! The prize itself was burned, after first giving the Southern gunners some practice.

For the next seventeen days 'Sumter' cruised steadily along the New York trade route, but only on the 5th of October was another ship sighted – and that British. Unfortunately, even that wasn't identified until after a long chase had occurred. The British had thought 'Sumter' a pirate vessel, and had tried to run for safety !

Turning south again, Semmes continued to find neutrals to chase, including on the 25th of October, a Prussian ship, which didn't recognise the Confederate colours – didn't know who the United States was fighting: all very frustrating for him. Semmes had indeed almost given up hope, when two days later, there appeared an American sailing ship, a schooner. This was the ' Daniel Trowbridge' from New York, carrying provisions and livestock for Demarara. After transferring from her huge hams, sides of bacon and much flour, together with the livestock, the prize was burned. 'Sumter' changed direction once more, cruising on a north-west course.

However, this proved another quiet time, with only neutral shipping seen. Semmes had been at sea now 57 days, needed more coal, so put in to the next harbour on his route, Martinique. There they were allowed to reprovision, but as all coal there belonged to the French government and could not be touched, 'Sumter' would eventually be obliged to move on to an available supply at the nearby island of St. Pierre. In the meantime they found Martinique a wonderfully hospitable place, being invited into homes and given a good welcome. There seemed much sympathy on the island for the Southern cause. Had not Frenchmen themselves just fought for their own freedom ?

While at Martinique Semmes received disquieting reports from Maranham. It was said that the U.S.S 'Powhatten' had arrived there just five days after 'Sumter' left, and her crew were talking about the recapture of 'Abby Bradford', one of 'Sumter's prizes. Apparently, the 'Powhatten' had been guarding the entrances to New Orleans on 13th of August, when that vessel appeared, trying to get into the river. 'Abby Bradford' had been stopped and taken. Greatly to the delight of the captors, she still carried papers relating to 'Sumter's probable course, and at once 'Powhatten' was assigned to the chase. On the 18th of August she was at Cienfuegos, on 21st Jamaica, and on the 29th heard of 'Sumter's movements at Curacao. As recently as the 21st of September 'Powhatten' had been at Maranham, on the Confederate's track, so could well be closing in on her. Semmes decided to cut short their holiday. He left immediately for St. Pierre and that coal.

It only took a few hours to get to their new destination, and once there, permission to refuel was readily given. 30 tons were loaded by nightfall.

November 14th dawned dull and drizzly, but provisioning continued apace aboard 'Sumter', where Captain Semmes watched anxiously for the 'Powhatten'. The sooner he could get away the better. As it happened, the 'Powhatten' was nowhere near Martinique, having gone directly back to New York, but his suspicions were fully justified. As 2.30 pm was striking on a local church clock, the 'U.S.S. Iroquois' came into view in the bay. Semmes could only look in horror, then give orders for action stations. 'Sumter' dropped her lighters and moved into the open water of the bay.

'Iroquois', of course, could not attack inside the harbour. Blockade she could, though, and after a few preliminary circles to investigate, she came to rest half a mile from 'Sumter'. The day passed in considerable tension.

How did she come to be there ? It seemed that the Federal ship had been at St. Thomas, another island not far away, when a messenger arrived in a hurry on the 12th of November, with news of the 'Sumter'. Leaving at once the American didn't take long to track her down.

Semmes found himself in a tricky position, unable to get away, yet unable to stay, for any delay would bring other warships to the scene. As for Captain Palmer of 'Iroquois', he felt certain of ultimate victory, provided he watched the 'Sumter' closely, because his was the faster and more powerful ship. He could wait; and in the meantime arranged for spies in the dockyard to give word of any movement. There was also an American merchant ship in port, herself locked up by 'Sumter's presence, but available to help in the watch. Flares were to be sent up by this vessel in the direction 'Sumter' took on leaving. All the while the French authorities took no action except to reinforce and ensure their neutral status was respected.

Nine days passed, and nine clear nights. There were no opportunities for Semmes. Then on the 23rd of November the skies clouded over, and when darkness came a moonless sky gave them a chance. 'Sumter' slipped anchor silently, and steamed quietly and swiftly - to the south. Unfortunately for them, shouting crowds on the quayside gave the game away, and at once green flares rose from the American merchantman, telling Captain Palmer to go south. 'Iroquois' hastened to the south end of the bay – and found nothing – 'Sumter' had swung north as soon as she was out of sight, steamed right past the north end of the bay, with no lights showing and her silhouette hidden against the hills. The manoeuvre had been successful.

Soon two more prizes were taken, as the raider steamed north. First was the 'Montmorency', a coal carrier, which, because she had a British cargo, was merely bonded on the 24th of November for $20,000. The schooner 'Arcade' was burned next day. By now, though, the sea was growing rough, and the wind was hard against them. 'Sumter' was really beginning to feel the pressure, too, of six months at sea, and was coming loose in every joint. After all, she had not been built for this type of work. Coal would run low presently, for by the end of the month there were only seven days supply left – even full bunkers held only 500 tons. Semmes decided to sail east for Europe, making use of the wind, and cutting back severely on coal use.

At once another ship was sighted on a converging course, heaving and pitching through the high waves, but clearly flying a United States flag. Semmes hoisted French colours, and, maintaining his trickery until close, had no difficulty in capturing the 'Vigilant', out of New York, but in ballast. She, too, was burned after transfer of crew.

The 8th of December brought still more stormy weather, and the worsening roll of the ship seemed to be starting leaks everywhere. Thus, they only just saw 'Ebenezer Dodge' through flying spray and gloom. Nevertheless, she was a good prize, being an American whaling ship en route to the fishing grounds, and therefore full of provisions. Having removed some of those supplies, the Confederates as usual destroyed her by fire.

A new problem for the cruise was the presence of so many prisoners – 43 in total to be fed and secured, and as enemies, all must be potential troublemakers. Semmes was particularly worried by the hostility of Captain Hoxie of the 'Ebenezer Dodge', because he lost no opportunity of complaining about 'Sumter'. According to him, the ship was filthy dirty, the crew mutinous. What was more, Semmes had confiscated from him $150, a sum he was never to see again – it being considered a legitimate prize of war, and he blamed Semmes for the death of his steward, who was already ill when transferred to Confederate custody. Captain Hoxie made Semmes feel extremely nervous.

The weather worsened. On the 11th of December lightning and thunder were in the background as sail was shortened to cope with increasing rain and heaving waves; there was a sudden crack as a stronger surge broke into 'Sumter's side near the bow. Water smashed straight into her hull. Repairs were hastily made, but conditions aboard had deteriorated as fast as the barometer reading fell. At 7.30 pm part of one spar blew away with its rigging. Now, to everyone's surprise the wind changed direction quickly, until the storm was blowing from the south – and still as strong as ever. This must be in the centre of a cyclone.

Eventually the wind abated somewhat, and 'Sumter' began to make progress, but that was merely a pause, and her mad plunging continued right through the month. By that time the sick list was alarmingly long, water was getting low, and the leaking was increasing. 'Sumter' must get into a port soon. In fact, though, they had almost completed their Atlantic crossing, and when those cyclone-like winds slowed down to a mere gale, thoughts turned instead to possibilities on the north-south trade routes near the coast. Perhaps some American shipping might be about. Indeed, when 35 sails were sighted on one day, the reality that none were American served only to raise hopes. Next day, however, the same thing happened. Where were those stars and stripes ? On that day, too, the gale began to regain its vigour, causing some damage to 'Sumter's propeller blades and shaft. A change of plan was obviously called for, and Semmes made for land, cutting across the sea lane. Cadiz light, rather further north than he expected, was made by 7 am on the morning of the 4th of January.

Any Confederate might have been worried about this landfall, because the Spanish authorities had never favoured 'Sumter' – remember those six prizes, handed back at Cienfuegos to the United States. It was really only out of necessity that they decided to land there.

Now, although the Spanish would have preferred not to see anything of 'Sumter', they were obliged by international agreement to allow her in and to have such repairs done as would enable her to go to sea again. So out came a pilot. However, they saw to it that she was taken right up river, ostensibly to where repairs could be better carried out, but also to keep her under observation. Semmes noticed, incidentally, as they passed through, that there were many American ships in harbour. Was that the fault of the weather or the close proximity of 'Sumter'?

Certainly many repairs were necessary. Dry dock was essential, too, because work on 'Sumter's false keel and forefoot were matters not to be neglected – even though the Spanish insisted that the minimum be done.

Semmes very soon began to have problems with his crew in Cadiz, no doubt the fault of city attractions and the growing inconvenience of their life as commerce raiders. Those other crews in port, mostly from merchant vessels, all seemed to be having a better life. On the 14th of January five of his men were missing, on the 15th another nine disappeared – and only two were recovered.

However, an abrupt Spanish order to leave was served on Semmes on the 16th, making it necessary to finish off repairs in temporary fashion. At least he need worry no more about the sailors. Actually, she left the quayside on the 17th just as a messenger arrived with conciliation in mind - 'Sumter' might stay one day more if required. But Semmes had been very much annoyed by his treatment, and left that messenger waving his papers on the quayside. He wouldn't stop. He would go straight to Gibraltar, a British port, where the reception ought to be a lot better.

Steaming south and feeling happier, Semmes resolved to make some trouble for the United States before he landed again. Indeed, he was lucky, for two prizes fell into his hands in one day, on the same evening of which he arrived in Gibraltar. Of the two, 'Neopolitan' was burned, while 'Investigator', carrying a Britain bound cargo, was released on bond, perhaps a sensible way to treat the last victim of 'Sumter's cruise.

After coming to rest in the harbour, Semmes went ashore to a warm welcome from the British, and probably to their surprise, requested the loan of an anchor – to replace the one left in St. Pierre.

'Sumter' now received a thorough examination; and perhaps many were relieved to hear that she was unseaworthy, in need of lengthy repairs. She would be in Gibraltar for many weeks. So much had really been obvious when the old ship began to leak all round her timbers after leaving Cadiz. Captain Semmes could not have been optimistic. Of course, such a man did not give up easily, and tried to enter with enthusiasm into the work ahead. He despatched one of his officers immediately to find and pay for more coal. There being insufficient in Gibraltar, the officer, Henry Myers, paymaster, set off for Cadiz to try to get some secretly. Unfortunately, this exercise worked against the Confederates, because Myers was arrested under an order of the United States consul at Tangier, while en route to Cadiz. He was eventually shipped back to America as a prisoner of war.

To carry misfortune further, three Federal warships arrived to stand off Gibraltar: the U.S.Ships 'Tuscarora', 'Kearsage' and 'Ino', all of whom could base themselves at nearby Algeciras. The 'Sumter' was well and truly blockaded, and this time there would be no escape.

On May 6th Semmes gave up. Judging by a letter he had recently written to the London Times, bitterly attacking the United States for piracy, and sneering at the failure of their navy to catch him, he was a man in need of a rest. The terrible Atlantic crossing and an unpleasant Spanish welcome must have had a dreadfully wearing effect, while the comparative shortness of his prize list must have been a disappointment. Yet he had accomplished much, and given a rest Semmes was the one the Confederate government looked to for a future command at sea – as will be narrated below.

'Sumter' was laid up, to await sale, while the crew was paid off. The officers, though, were Confederate servicemen, and they would go into the newly formed pool of naval talent in Europe, from which future commerce raiders might be staffed. Indeed, the career of 'Sumter' had shown that the Confederate policy of using whatever ships they could find in the Southern ports had run its course. 'Nashville' and 'Sumter' had been successful, to a point, but were only viable before the Unites States Navy became properly organised, with modern ships. The Confederacy would have to match those with modern vessels of their own, and given the absence of a shipbuilding industry in the South, could get them from foreign manufacture alone – that is, in Europe.

Note 1 – Extract from Raphael Semmes' letter to the Times of London in June 1864, concerning the fate of those six prizes.

"The cargoes of several of these vessels were claimed, as appeared by certificates found among the papers, as Spanish property. This fact cannot, of course, be verified, except by a judicial proceeding in the prize courts of the Confederate States. But while this fact is being determined what is to be done with the property ? I have the right to destroy the vessels, but not the cargoes, in case the latter should prove to be, as claimed, Spanish property; but how can I destroy the former and not the latter ? I cannot before sentence unlade the cargoes and deliver them to the complainant, for I do not know that the claims will not be sustained. Indeed, one of the motives which influenced me in seeking a Spanish port, was the fact that these cargoes were claimed by Spanish subjects, whom I am desirous of putting to as little inconvenience as possible in the unloading and reception of their property after sentence, in case it should be restored to them.".

PRIZE LIST OF C.S.S. SUMTER

Name	Home Port	Type	Cargo	Date taken	Result
'Golden Rocket'	Maine		Ballast	3rd July 1861	Burned
'Cuba'	Maine	Brigantine	Sugar	4th "	Retaken
'Machias'	Maine	"	"	4th "	"
'Ben Dunning'	New York	"	"	4th "	"
'Albert Adams'	New York	"	"	4th "	"
'Louisa Kilham'		"	"	5th "	"
'West Wind'		"	"	5th "	"
'Naiad'		"	"	5th "	"
'Abby Bradford'	New York	Schooner	Provs	25th July	Recapt.
'Joseph Maxwell'	Philadelphia	Barque		27th "	Retaken
'Joseph Parke'		Brigantine	Ballast	25th Sept	Burned
'Daniel Trowbridge'	Newhaven	Schooner	Provs	27th Oct	Burned
'Montmorency'			Coal	25th Nov	Bonded $20,000
'Arcade'	Portland	Schooner	Molasses	26th "	Burned
'Vigilant'	Maine		Ballast	3rd Dec	Burned
'Ebenezer Dodge'	New Bedford	Whaler	Provs	8th "	Burned
'Neopolitan'	Kingston	Barque	Fruit	18th Jan 1862	Burned
'Investigator'	Maine	Barque	Ore	18th Jan "	Bonded $15,000

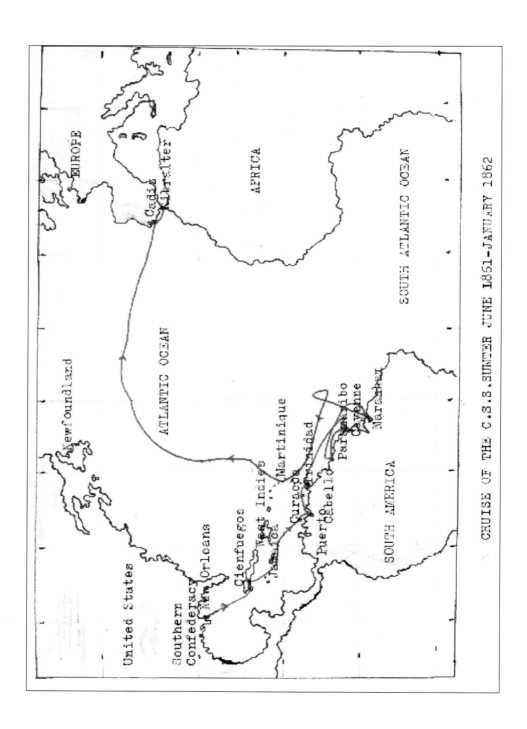

CRUISE OF THE C.S.S.SUMTER JUNE 1861-JANUARY 1862

CHAPTER FOUR

The Move To Liverpool

The Confederates had tried privateers, with limited success, but by the end of 1861 that initiative had been completely frustrated by the blockade. They had tried seizing ships in Southern ports, but those found were few in number and proved rather unsuitable for conversion to commerce raiding. If, therefore, the South was to have an effective presence at sea, new ships of special design would have to be built, and built somewhere abroad, because there were no shipbuilding facilities in the Confederacy. Where should they look ? The choice, after due consideration, was Liverpool, that busy port and prominent shipbuilding centre, where the South already had good connections through the cotton trade – Liverpool, in a neutral country and therefore a risky option, yet where active sympathy for their cause was expected. How could they have been so confident ? The answer surely turned on relations between The United States and Great Britain.

In 1812 the two countries had been at war, and for years afterwards there had been mutual suspicion and dislike: indeed, many differences were essentially long term, and still in place in 1860. Canada was one problem, where Britain feared American expansionism, and through which country the United States saw American recruits for Britain's war in the Crimea being channelled. Another problem, strangely enough, was with the slave trade. Britain was actively trying to stop slave ships from Africa, and was somewhat frustrated by those carrying the American flag, which could not be touched. Nevertheless, in the period just before 1860 matters overall had been improving, with trade developing well, especially the exchange of Southern cotton for manufactured goods. Relations had improved to the point that The United States felt Britain would certainly remain neutral in case of war – would not interfere in the affairs of the South.

However, in 1860 the United States Congress introduced a new bill, to be known by its sponsor's name thereafter as the Morrill tariff. This placed heavy duties on manufactured goods from abroad, and was of course, designed to protect American industry. The bill was passed in February 1861. At once the the South felt at a disadvantage, because their trade in cotton for manufactures was so important; and naturally foreign manufacturers selling to the South, especially Britain, were upset. Here was a common cause for both, which could only add to the fear that civil war in America would lead to a cotton famine in Europe. In 1860 fully 80% of Britain's cotton imports were from America. If war came, Britain would be well advised to recognise the South as a separate country, following which any blockade of Southern ports could be broken and trade continue as before.

Add to this feeling the sense that " If the Southerners want their freedom, why should they not have it ?" - a sentiment definitely fashionable in 1860. Add also the idea that property owning gentlemen in England, many of whom were in the government, had much more understanding of their counterparts in the South, in spite of slavery, than they had of Northern democrats: the reason for a general sympathy toward the South among that social class in 1861 is apparent. In that atmosphere, old and outstanding differences soon surfaced again. Misunderstandings would easily arise.

On May 13th 1861, in reply to President Lincoln's declaration that Southern privateers must be considered pirates, the British minister for foreign affairs, Earl Russell gave out that England would recognise the equal rights of Confederate ships and would help neither side in any outstanding case. This essentially recognised the Confederates as a belligerent power, and though stopping short of treating them as a nation, it did defy the United States resolution that the Southern states were merely rebelling against authority. Russell's announcement was quickly followed by another, stating that the Confederates had every right to prey on United States merchant shipping, if their ships were commanded by Confederate naval officers, and that British sailors were entitled to serve on those vessels, if they wished. All these remarks were made just before Charles Adams, the United States representative, arrived in London to discuss Britain's neutrality – hardly a friendly beginning.

When Britain next asked each belligerent to recognise formally the Declaration of Paris, made in 1856 (and discussed in Chapter One), it was merely pouring salt on open wounds. The United States had not signed this agreement, which was intended to abolish privateering as a legal instrument of war. Indeed, they retained the right to privateer. Equally, the Confederates, who had not signed either, were entitled to use the same weapon. As they were the only belligerent with a target to aim for, the situation largely favoured them. On the other hand, if the United States were at war with Britain, they could not privateer against that country without incurring the wrath of the many other countries who had, along with Britain, signed the treaty. Thus the United States lost both ways, and grew vociferous in criticising the British government.

In fact Russell was correct in his appreciation of the situation, and was still trying to remain neutral, even allowing for any pro-Southern sympathy. How could anyone treat the navy of a people five million strong as pirates ? In time that point of view came to be discerned, even in America, as the difference between belligerency and independence was realised.

A further cause for friction was, as anticipated, cotton. The blockade of Southern ports quickly cut down the amount of cotton leaving the Confederacy, and European shipowners fought back through blockade running. Suitably prepared ships, grey or black painted steamers with low profiles, operating mostly from the British colonies of Bermuda and The Bahama Islands, plyed in and out of the Confederacy. Medicines, arms, ammunition and other necessities of war were delivered to the colonies by regular merchantmen, then transferred to blockade runners in exchange for cotton. Large profits were made: and unsurprisingly, those colonial ports were united in their pro-Southern bent.

It is worth mentioning that the Confederates thought the cotton shortage would bring Britain into the war on their side. They were wrong, firstly because in 1861 English warehouses contained about two years supply, giving time for deliveries from India and Egypt to be arranged. Even when the Lancashire mills did run short, and many workers had to be laid off temporarily, there existed a sympathy among those men for the anti-slavery cause. There was little trouble, in spite of the disruption.

Determined to keep the peace with America, Earl Russell would not agree to break the Southern blockade, something France wanted, and complaints about the 'Sumter' breaking neutrality laws in Trinidad were followed by a British order that "..in British ports belligerent ships were to remain twenty-four hours only in necessity; that no more coal was to be supplied than would carry them to their nearest home port; and that after coaling, the same ship must not refuel again in a British port for a period of three months". That the rule was broken so often during the war, especially in colonial ports, was certainly bound to annoy the United States, but was sincerely meant.

In fact, the nearest Britain came to war in 1861 was in the matter of the 'Trent'. The Confederates sent two men to represent their government in Europe, Messrs. Mason and Slidell, the former destined for England, the latter for France. They left by blockade runner, and transferred to the British ship, 'Trent'. On November 8th that steamer was intercepted by the Union warship 'San Jacinto', the two men being forcibly removed and delivered to the United States. At the time the North was badly in need of a hero, and Captain Wilkes of the 'San Jacinto' was loudly acclaimed everywhere. In Britain, of course, the response was rather different, and protests about this behaviour were strong and threatening. In the end President Lincoln had personally to back down and release the Confederates, but it all made for bad feeling.

To summarise, relations between the United States and Britain had become strained in 1861. Americans generally at the beginning of the war felt Britain wanted to support the South. Matters since then had only got worse, in their view, and it was suspected that Britain would at least like to recognise the Confederacy as a separate country, if not join it to fight the North. On the other hand, from the British perspective, there was no wish to get into hostilities. Recognition might come, but not yet, and Britain would remain a sympathetic neutral.

That situation was sufficiently promising for the Confederate government to look to England first for naval requirements. (France also played its part, but that story will come later). Great care and secrecy would be needed in a neutral country, but the notion of passive support might be relied upon to see things through; that, and the backing of large amounts of Confederate money.

As it happened, the men for the job were soon to hand. Samuel Barron was chosen for France – more of him later – and James D. Bulloch seemed ideal for the mission to Liverpool.

Bulloch had been a ship's captain, and applied to Stephen Mallory for a seagoing task. He was a real Southern patriot, an able and intelligent man, yet who had shown loyalty and honesty at the beginning of the war, when captain of a merchant ship caught in a Southern port. He had insisted that the ship be returned to its Northern owners, and had indeed done so personally, before joining the Confederates in Richmond. Mallory was certainly impressed. Integrity would be needed for the work to come, because as Confederate agent Bulloch would be almost entirely independent, and at the same time handling large amounts of their money.

James Bulloch arrived in Liverpool on June 4th 1861 and went into action immediately. Working from his hotel room, he quietly ordered two ships from Liverpool builders, and arranged for Confederate cash to pay for them. The latter was to be through Fraser and Trenholm Ltd. of 10 Rumford Place, Liverpool, a Charleston company specialising in the sale of cotton, and with other branches conveniently in Bermuda and Nassau (there known as Adderley and Co). Becoming now an arm of the Confederate government, this company was used right through the war and their money supply never failed.

Bulloch returned temporarily to the Confederacy in November, but finally settled into an office at Fraser and Trenholm in Liverpool by February 1862. He worked closely with Charles Prioleau, the manager of F. and T., whose English home was at 19 Abercrombie Square, Liverpool.

It is still possible to see the Star of South Carolina over that doorway.

From Fawcett, Preston and Co. of Liverpool, Bulloch ordered an iron screw gunboat, to be of 700 tons, bark rigged but with two smoke stacks. The ship's hull was actually made by Miller and Son, also in Liverpool, but afterwards was completed by the first named company. She was to be known as the 'Oreto', and it was given out that she was to be registered in Britain, to travel on a run to Palermo, then to be delivered to Italian owners in that port. The pretence of being a merchant ship was to avoid the British Foreign Enlistment Act, by which the Queen's subjects could not build, arm or equip vessels of war for use against nations friendly to Britain. Guns and ammunition would be sent out separately by Bulloch, and transferred to 'Oreto' at sea. A Captain Duguid was engaged to take her out as a merchantman, and he signed articles to that effect. By the beginning of March 1862, 'Oreto' was coaled up, provisioned and ready to leave.

Now the British authorities, both in Liverpool and London, were suspicious of her destination from the start, for they realised Bulloch had not long arrived from the Confederacy. The United States too were on the watch, having established their own agents in Liverpool. The builders must, of course, have known what was going on, because their ship had gun sockets, shot racks, powder tanks and provisions for four months. Given guns and ammunition 'Oreto' could have been prepared for battle in 24 hours. In fact it was openly rumoured all the way through her construction that 'Oreto' was going out as a Confederate cruiser, and although Liverpool was staunchly pro-South, those rumours soon reached the United States Consul, Thomas Dudley. He demanded action, on the grounds 'Oreto' was a warship. If the rumours were proved correct, Britain would have to act to stop the ship.

But proof was difficult to obtain. Here is the report of a customs officer, Edward Morgan, appointed to check over the ship.

"I am one of the surveyors of customs at this port. Pursuant to instructions I received from the Collector on the 21st February 1862, and at subsequent dates, I visited the steamer 'Oreto' at various times, when she was being fitted out in the dock, close to the yard of Messrs. Miller and Son, the builder of the vessel. I continued this inspection from time to time until she left the dock, and I am certain that she had no warlike stores on board. After she went into the river she was constantly watched by the boarding officer, who was directed to report to me whenever any goods were taken on board; but in reply to my frequent enquiries, he stated that nothing was put into the ship but coals". Truly he must have been turning a blind eye. Nevertheless, following this and other reports, nothing could be done to stop 'Oreto' leaving, even though the Italian consul protested ignorance of the connection with his country.

Thus 'Oreto' left Liverpool on the 22nd of March 1862, and eventually arrived at Nassau in the Bahama Islands to become the Confederate cruiser 'Florida'. Perhaps it is reasonable to suggest that a more detailed enquiry in Liverpool might have revealed her true purpose.

Just as blatant was the case of Ship 290 (also unofficially known as the 'Enrica'), the second cruiser ordered by Bulloch, and being built by Lairds and Co. in Birkenhead. Although this, too, was stated to be a merchant vessel, word had it that she was for Confederate service. Now, given the experience with 'Oreto', it should have been very quickly stopped: Dudley was swift enough to present his case through Charles Adams in London. From there the neutral foreign secretary Earl Russell immediately referred it back to Liverpool. Unless the vessel was definitely shown not to be for the Confederates, she should be detained, and fitting out suspended. However, the port Collector of Customs, who had allowed 'Oreto' to escape, was consistent with his previous decision. He returned the papers to London, stating that.." in all certainty 290 was not for the South", and advising Russell to give up the enquiry – though he himself would continue to watch the ship.

Adams would not accept defeat, and neither did Dudley in Liverpool. His spies combed the waterfront bars for information, while a solicitor was employed to bring the whole case together. Eventually he had the signed affidavits of six witnesses, who could show that Ship 290 was indeed a Confederate cruiser. By now, though, it was the 21st of July 1862, and 290 nearly ready. When those same Customs officials in Liverpool declared the 'proof' unacceptable in law, Adams rushed to employ a London barrister, Sir Robert Collier. But even his opinion that 290 should be stopped failed to sway anyone in Liverpool. Adams now went straight to Russell, with his papers, from whose office the law officers of the Crown were consulted. Things began to happen. On 23rd July the proofs went to Queen's Advocate Alan Harding for a decision. Unfortunately he fell ill the same day, did not return to work for five more, and all that time the papers lay on his desk. Finally, on 28th July the order was given to seize 290 – too late, for, guided by her temporary captain, Butcher, she sailed that day, soon to become the cruiser 'Alabama'.

By so dragging their feet, Britain's government had not impressed Adams or Dudley. Perhaps Russell was correct in his cautious and painstaking approach, but the United States definitely sensed a bias against them in 1862: and were justified in that opinion when 'Florida' and 'Alabama' began to disrupt American shipping across the world. Many merchant ships were for their own protection re-registered under the British flag in the next two years, a nice increase in revenue for the United Kingdom. Yet more evidence of partiality came from the use of British colonial ports for coaling and provisioning, something which continued almost until the end of the war – all in breach of the clear policy of their government.

Through 1862 the Confederates' luck held. James Bulloch was able to sell 'Sumter', laid up in Gibraltar, using released funds for future purchases. On January 10th, 1863, another ship built for him on the Clyde, as far from Liverpool as might deflect suspicion, was launched under the name 'Virginia'. She went on to become the cruiser 'Georgia', a third active commerce raider.

Evident favouring of the South had depended to a large extent on its military success and likely independence. Most of 1862 passed with those probabilities intact. However, by the end of the year the balance had changed, and the North was seen to be winning. With it came a subtle shift in foreign, especially British, sentiment. Suddenly, people became more conscious of slavery in the South and its wrongs, while Charles Adams was able to report from London by January 1863 that "Public opinion is with us": and that made life in Liverpool much more difficult for Bulloch.

The 'Alexandra' was ordered by the Confederates in late 1862, and was to be on the model of 'Oreto'. She was launched on 7th of March 1863, but by then the Thomas Dudley spy network had done its job, and a report was speedily placed before the British government. 'Alexandra' was detained. As it turned out, and after a lengthy trial, ending with a verdict of guilt unproven, she was released. However, the case remained as a precedent, on which all future similar prosecutions could be based. Seizure and trial of this vessel had been a correct action on behalf of the United States, one which might justifiably have occurred even earlier. The 'Alexandra' herself was released too late to be of any use as a raider, and was employed instead as a blockade runner until the dissolution of the Confederacy.

Another interesting affair was that of the 'Pampero', being built on the Clyde for Bulloch, and seized in November 1863. To avoid the trouble experienced with 'Alexandra', the nominal owners allowed the prosecution to win without opposition, with the promise 'Pampero' would not be sold for two years. Their scheme was to sell her to the Confederates after the two years, and was apparently quite sound, except that there was no Confederacy left by then.

From the middle of 1863 on it became extremely difficult for James Bulloch to operate in Britain, even though all his transactions were kept secret. That the United States gained from the new situation is obvious, considering the two ships 'Pampero' and 'Alexandria', and the abortive matter of the Laird rams, ordered in Liverpool in 1863. The latter were armoured steamships with projecting steel rams, their design quite new and specifically for destruction of the Southern blockade. Undoubtedly they would have been successful, too, if let loose. Fortunately for the United States, they were arrested permanently before completion.

Lairds also built quite a number of ships destined to be blockade runners, including the 'Penguin' for Charles Prioleau personally. Yet they denied in all cases a connection with the Confederacy – and nothing was ever proved.

Charles Adams and Thomas Dudley had between them brought a halt to the building of Confederate ships in Britain. However, Bulloch could still buy, and money was available to him. In November 1863 he found the 'Victor' lying in the Thames, a naval despatch boat and comparatively new, but no longer required by a modernising British navy. The 'Victor' was quietly bought by a local company and on 10th November secretly handed over to the Confederates. Adams had no suspicions at first; but rumours flew about as ever, and the sight of 'Victor' being fitted with very unfreighter-like appurtenances at Sheerness, was quite enough. She was indeed a fine ship, painted black like all the cruisers, and well capable of being another 'Alabama'. Adams wasted no time, was in fact almost ready to make his move, when Bulloch just got in first. Although the masts, rigging and tanks were all in mid-process, and workmen were still aboard, the order to leave at once arrived. So away went the 'Victor', carrying her protesting builders, without arms and many necessities. In the channel she met a tender sent out by Bulloch, and Confederate officers changed places with the workmen. 'Victor' was renamed 'Rappahannock', and for the fourth time a Confederate flag flew over a cruiser supplied in Britain.

However, 'Rappahannock' was a cruiser only in name. Much boiler work needed to be done, and her coal bunkers were more or less empty. Very few crew members had arrived. Circumstances made a risk inevitable: she immediately put into Calais, where the authorities were still overriding neutrality to help the South. More of 'Rappahannock's story will be disclosed in due course.

The struggle in Britain between the representatives of North and South never ceased as long as the war in America was going on. From 1863 the United States played its advantage, manifested by the seizure of various blockade runners in private hands – not being built by the Confederate government. Some of those vessels were released for lack of evidence, others legally prevented from sailing. Bulloch went his own way in the meantime, and did, in fact, have one more success, again by purchase.

The United States Consul at Liverpool, Thomas Dudley, was the first to notice the 'Sea King' being built. That was late in 1863, but he could see in her the raider of the future, strong and sleek enough to be another 'Alabama'. He reported the work going on to Charles Adams. But 'Sea King' turned out to be a legitimate merchant vessel, built for the India trade, and his case was dropped.

Dudley was right to be suspicious. There was no ship in Britain at that time to compare with the power, the beauty and the latent strength of the 'Sea King', an auxiliary steamer that averaged 17 knots under full power.

She could sail for months without the use of steam and was as fast as any craft afloat. The maximum 12 knots of 'Florida' and 13 of 'Alabama' seemed obsolete beside her.

Unsurprisingly, then, James Bulloch was delighted to hear that 'Sea King' was up for sale, soon after its return from a first trip to Bombay. By now it was September 1864, the Confederacy was struggling, yet they had a chance here to buy a cruiser finer than the 'Alabama'. However, great care was needed. Everyone was watching, no word of interest must escape. In secret Bulloch arranged for one Richard Wright, distantly related to a Southern gentleman, but quite unknown in England, to purchase 'Sea King' in his own name, then to hand her over to a Mr. Corbett – ostensibly an innocent merchant captain. Corbett would resell while at sea to certain Confederates brought across by other means.

The secret was well kept, for nothing leaked to the ever-vigilant representatives of the United States. Even so, Adams ordered two Union warships, the 'Niagara' and 'Sacramento' to search 'Sea King' when she came out: these two were actually in the Thames estuary, for all the world on blockade duty. In fact, when the 'Sea King' did sail down the channel the Americans failed to recognise her, and the fifth and last Confederate ship provided from British waters went on to become the commerce raider 'Shenandoah'. Her story is told in Chapter Thirteen.

The American Civil War was over by May 1865. The Confederacy had been utterly defeated, leaving James Bulloch and his colleagues in Europe to pick up the pieces left by their separate but determined campaign. Bulloch collected all the Southerners he could find and managed to repatriate them to America, but fearing prosecution himself, decided in the end not to go back. He settled down in Canning Street, Liverpool, earned a living by some small business ventures, and dying there in 1901, was buried in Toxteth cemetery.

Bulloch could certainly have claimed that, from his point of view, the mission to Liverpool had been a success. In the early part of the war, when local feeling was on his side, he had built and sent out the two most successful commerce raiders owned by the Confederates, 'Alabama' and 'Florida'. Later, as opinions of the South changed, 'Georgia' and 'Shenandoah' were squeezed through all the obstacles, and became an undeniable nuisance to their opposition. Amidst those successes only 'Rappahannock' failed to make a worthwhile contribution.

However, for now a British measure of their achievement will suffice. It is from the speech made by Milner Gibson, President of the British Board of Trade, on January 20th 1864.

"The number of British ships entering in and clearing out cargoes in the United Kingdom has increased in the present year to an amount of something like 14,000,000 tons against 7,000,000 tons foreign. Much of this is due to the transference of carrying-trade from United States to British ships. And why ? There is the fear amongst U.S. merchant shipping of attack by certain armed vessels that are careering over the ocean. The decrease in the employment of U.S. shipping is about 46-47%. What might happen to this country, with her commerce, if she went to war with some nation that availed herself of these methods ?"

The British government did try, especially from 1863 on, to maintain a completely neutral stance. But it had much to answer for. British and colonial ports had been used as Southern bases, in which the utmost hospitality had been offered to Southern sailors. (Indeed, without those harbours the Confederate cruisers could hardly have functioned at all). They had effectively allowed a branch of the Confederate government, whose country was never recognised here, to set up on their own soil, and had protected considerable numbers of blockade runners under their own flag. Lastly, they had enforced a strict neutrality upon United States vessels, thus establishing a definite bias, which was, unfortunately, quite open.

All this was deeply resented by the United States, and led to the famous 'Alabama claims case', convened in Geneva in 1871, and settled in 1872 with an award to the United States of over £3,000,000 ($15,500,000) for damage to the U.S. merchant marine caused through British negligence or active cooperation: and Britain paid.

CHAPTER FIVE

'Florida' & 'Alabama' in 1862

In spite of the controversy which attended the departure of 'Oreto', one could not but admire such a ship, a thoroughbred of the seas. Her low, black painted hull, her double funnels and swept-back superstructure made her a work of art, whose attraction was much more than functional efficiency. 'Oreto' had an overall weight of 1,500 tons and a full complement of crew would be 135 men.

Like 'Alabama' after her, but unlike 'Sumter' before, this vessel was designed with long ocean trips in mind. She was not so much dependent on a mixture of sail and steam, being able to proceed quite satisfactorily on one or other alone; a big advantage. It had been relatively easy to follow the course of 'Sumter', for she was ever calling in at foreign ports for fuel and necessities her tanks and holds couldn't manage. 'Oreto', in contrast, might disappear into the oceans for weeks together, existing on large reserves and frustrating any pursuer.

On the 22nd March 1862, 'Oreto' left Liverpool under the control of Captain Duguid, directed first to call at Nassau in the Bahamas (on her way to Italy, it was announced, and a ship might just do that without arousing suspicion). She carried only 52 seamen, of whom just one was American. Simultaneously the 'Bahama', a merchantman, left Hartlepool in England under Captain Tessier, with a cargo of guns and equipment, also bound for Nassau. Both ships flew the British ensign.

If the fine weather gave 'Oreto' an uneventful maiden voyage, at least part of the satisfaction was due to her excellent performance. She would burn on the average 42 tons of coal a day, giving a steady speed of 9.5 knots, while under sail alone she could make 12. 'Oreto' and 'Bahama' arrived at Nassau within a few days of each other, to be met by the Confederate agent Heyliger, and for 'Oreto' to receive her new captain; Duguid being relieved by John N. Maffitt and his officers. To supply experience the latter included John Stribling of 'Sumter'. Others were

Samuel W. Averatt, first officer, J.L.Hoole, C.W.Read and S.G.Stone.

Unfortunately the next thing to happen was the desertion by most of her British crew, who, being suspicious of 'Oreto's destination, had no great desire to serve on a foreign warship. Worse still, the British naval vessel 'Greyhound' swung alongside 'Oreto's anchorage, six miles from Nassau, and her Captain Hickley came aboard. He had information from the deserting seamen, it seems, that the new arrival was a Confederate cruiser, or was destined to become one, and the whole ship must be examined for a report to the authorities. Hickley was clearly no Southern sympathiser, and he quickly recommended the arrest of 'Oreto' with the remainder of her crew – 22 in all.

At first the Colonial Governor would not cooperate, in spite of protests from the United States consul, but on 7th June both 'Oreto' and 'Bahama' were brought into Nassau. Then, on the 17th they were released again, as the tussle continued. Not to be beaten, Captain Hickley kept up his complaints. Finally, re-arrest was ordered. The future was now very uncertain, because this decision made court action unavoidable. Luckily, few people agreed with Captain Hickley. Many witnesses were called, whose testimony tended only to cloud the issue, and the trial dragged on through July, with a friendly court making light of what appeared to be damning evidence for the Crown: and in the end came acquittal.

These were anxious days for Maffitt – who, surprisingly, had not been asked to speak at the trial. Five months had passed already since 'Oreto' had left Liverpool, five months without success. Maffitt lacked the tact or understanding of a Semmes, and his was never a popular ship, but he was a leader, a man of determined and unbending character, who wouldn't give up easily. He was an ardent Southern patriot, of course, another ex-navy officer, and before the war had been employed on the coastal survey, having been especially involved in the marking of Charleston's shipping channel. Now the acquittal gave him his opportunity at last. Maffitt took the 'Oreto' out of Nassau, ostensibly a merchant ship bound for St. Johns, Newfoundland, but actually only travelling as far as Green Cay, about 80 miles to the south. There he cleared decks and waited for 'Bahama'.

Of course, after what had gone before, unfriendly eyes in Nassau were on the 'Bahama' – what was her role to be ? The agent knew that if she left harbour, unwelcome attention would follow. So he resorted to off-loading her and repacking the cargo into a handy and well-known blockade runner, 'Prince Alfred'. Thus it appeared that after all, those guns and fittings aboard were intended for a Confederate port, and no further interest was paid in them – blockade running was a respectable pastime in Nassau, and it was to everyone's advantage that it should continue. The 'Prince Alfred' steamed away alone, and came to 'Oreto' in Green Cay.

At once work started on the transfer. Ports were readied, guns hoisted across, and ammunition lockers piled high with shells. It was only after the two 7 inch rifles and six 6 inch guns were in place, that Maffitt began to notice the absence of many detailed items in the 'Prince Alfred' cargo. It was true: in her hurry the blockade runner had left behind such indispensable units as rammers and sponges, and until these were made good, the 'Oreto's fighting equipment was useless. There was no question of going back for them; they would just have to move on, in the hope that sooner or later some of the vital necessities could be scrounged from somewhere. Just now it was time for the naming ceremony.

Imagine the scene in Green Cay as for the first time Confederate colours rose to the peak of the newly christened 'Florida'. The elegant grey uniforms of the officers, contrasting with the blue and white of ordinary seamen, but every man standing to attention in the sunlight, so emotionally conscious of the moment when Maffitt saluted his new command. A single cannon shot snapped out.

Salutes were returned by 'Prince Alfred's' crew dipping their flag, as they pulled away, and the spell was broken. 'Florida' was a fully fledged Confederate cruiser, and alone she would be for her active life.

The first concern for Maffitt had to be his shortage of crew and equipment. Cuba was not far away, and somewhere in Cuba was a Confederate agent. 'Florida' made for Cardenas on the north coast. Once there First Lt. Stribling went ashore, but finding nobody helpful, proceeded to Havana, where the Confederate agent was reported to be: a good move, surely, for the agent quickly assembled twelve volunteer seamen and a variety of stores for 'Florida' . Very unfortunately, those twelve men brought yellow fever into the ship, and even before the voyage could commence again, the crew started to fall ill. Maffitt was almost the first, and although his life was saved by an alert surgeon, Doctor Gilliard, in Havana, he became nearly helpless and certainly unable to captain his ship effectively.

However, he could still talk and think. It was apparent that the first cruise of 'Florida' would have to written off as a failure. There was nothing to show for it but a half-deserted deck and a litter of sick bodies. What must they do ? Neutrals would hardly wish to help a yellow fever ship, even if they approved of Confederates. They must run for a Southern port, and that straight away, before any United States warship was on hand. Mobile, Alabama, was the nearest friendly port, and, in spite of a considerable blockade fleet, would have to be attempted. Maffitt ordered John Stribling to take command and to go for Mobile. It was the beginning of September.

At Mobile were three blockading warships, the 'Oneida', flagship of the group, and under command of Captain Preble, the 'Winona' and the 'Rachel Seaman'. For many months they had been in position, in constant view of Fort Morgan, whose guns protected the approach to Mobile harbour. They had seen plenty of action, because blockade runners were frequently chancing the run in. Some of them were caught, some escaped, but whatever happened the blockade vigil was conscientiously maintained. So, when on September 4th the cry of 'Sail ho !' went up, it was all in a day's work. The oncoming sail was identified as a British warship, not surprisingly, since 'Florida' had a British design and was flying the British ensign. Seemingly she had come to inspect the blockade, and only 'Oneida' got under way to approach her. In fact 'Winona' was distracted by another sail just then, and moved away from the immediate vicinity. As it transpired, and although the US navy knew 'Florida' was about, they did not suspect she would try to go into Mobile, and had not, therefore, informed the blockading fleet of that possibility. Nor was it particularly unusual for a British steamer to enter Mobile – neutral warships had the right, provided they got permission from the blockade commander; and that was why 'Oneida' moved to intercept her.

On swept the stranger, while Captain Preble shaped his course to pass close to her. Then 'Florida' swerved to avoid the American, at the same time dropping her British flag. Recovering from his surprise, Preble hailed the ship, though he was still amazed to see no colours hoisted and hardly anyone on deck. Next he fired a shot across the bows, but to no effect. "Fire into her" was the order for 'Oneida' and with the other two blockaders just getting interested, shots began to splash around 'Florida'. Soon, indeed, damage was visible, but obviously superficial, for 'Florida' held her straight course for the protection of Fort Morgan – the blockade had been defeated.

Aboard the cruiser, however, the situation was painfully chaotic. Only three men remained fit, one of whom was John Stribling. He commanded and held the wheel throughout their run in, never deviating ; a truly gallant action. The quartermaster had lost his fingers pulling down the British flag, and that was why 'Florida' flew no colours at all from then on. Shells were hitting hard, one crashing through her side to shatter cabins and part of the berth deck. Another lodged in the coal bunkers without exploding. 'Florida' was really lucky to reach safety.

Once in Mobile and under inspection, it was obvious that several months would pass before the cruiser would be ready again. Repairs were needed, the sick men would have to recover, more crew would have to be recruited. It must have appeared that 'Florida' had done little in 1862 to further the cause of Southern independence. But in the world away from Mobile the prestige of 'Florida' had grown from her blockade run. Her next move would be awaited with some concern.

In the meantime, what had become of that other escapee from Liverpool: ship 290 ? Remember that she had only left port on the very day her arrest was announced. At the time a party had been going on aboard, and many guests, including ladies, had been there at the invitation of Captain Butcher. The idea, of course, was to deceive onlookers as to her readiness for sea. Then, while collective guards were down, a Liverpool tug suddenly approached, took off the visitors, and 290 was off.

From Britain too, another steamer called 'Agrippina' left almost simultaneously with a cargo of stores and guns. Ostensibly a merchant ship, her mission was to rendezvous with 290 at Terceira, in the Azores.

'Agrippina' had been purchased in London by James Bulloch. It had proved relatively easy to load her with those suitable stores without arousing suspicion, and to hire Alexander McQueen as captain. Indeed, Bulloch intended her for a second role as coaling ship to the Confederate cruisers, bringing best quality fuel from Cardiff.

Far away in Nassau, Raphael Semmes and other officers from Europe, especially from 'Sumter', had made themselves available to the 'Bahama', for her return voyage.

She, too, headed for the Azores.

Meanwhile, the port authorities of Liverpool had become thoroughly aroused, had informed the United States representatives, and the telegraph was humming with orders to stop 290. Even now she might have been caught, because the U.S.S.'Tuscarora' was in the vicinity, and was instructed to sweep the Irish Sea. For the benefit of this story, it is well to report that nothing was found by 'Tuscarora'. 290 arrived at Porto Praya, Terceira, on 10th August 1862, after an uneventful journey.

On the island, Butcher and his men received the kindest hospitality. Terceira was Portuguese, with plenty of good land, and in spite of being rather off the beaten track, was well populated. But the Confederate officers were permanently on edge, expecting at any time to see an unfriendly warship, and that with their ship still lying unarmed and helpless. So it was a great relief when 'Agrippina' arrived on the 18th August, immediately taking up a position near 290. Transfer of supplies began by small boat. Two days later 'Bahama' also reached Terceira, and the three ships moved to a secluded bay, away from the curiosity of the people of Porto Praya. There 'Agrippina' was lashed to 290, and the business of transfer continued in earnest.

This well kept rendezvous was probably the best exercise in coordination ever performed by the C.S.N.

When Semmes saw the ship he was to captain, he was positively thrilled. She was no 'Sumter', not at all. That vessel had acquired an important reputation, yet really she was no better than a tubby merchantman. 290, in contrast, looked something special, designed for speed and grace – she could reach 15 knots under combined sail and steam. Semmes liked the smooth symmetrical lines, the barquentine rigged upper works, the long masts, wire ropes and wide spread of her lower canvas. Walking below decks, over the entire 220 feet length, he could admire the elegance of her cabins, and the luxury of a suite of staterooms. All facilities were arranged to the greatest convenience of the crew, a credit to the designer's skill.

On the superstructure 290 carried five boats, a cutter, launch amidships, with gig and whaleboat a little aft, and a dingy at the stern. The deck was pierced for twelve guns, though only eight were shipped, and here was placed the hundred pound Blakeley rifle, pivoted forward, one eight inch solid shot gun, also pivoted, but aft, six thirty-two pound broadside guns, while magazine and shellroom were in closely convenient positions. Last of all below was 290's secret weapon, her water condenser for converting seawater into fresh, as a result of which the ship could remain for long periods completely out of sight of land and self-supporting. Semmes could eagerly slap the polished, simple-spoked wheel with delight, and praise the motto cut deep into its wood: "Aide Toi et Dieu t'aidera". Nor was he alone in admiration. Crew and officers together were equally excited.

By the 24th August everything had been done: transfers complete, decks washed down, and last supplies of fresh vegetables brought aboard. The three ships put out to sea, ready for the christening ceremony. The crews of all three ships lined up on parade in 290.

Semmes now approached the really tricky part of his work. Here he had just created a warship. Yet every sailor aboard had signed on a cargo steamer, and would have to be persuaded to join the Confederate navy. He could rely on the officers, of course – they were already of the C.S.N. Some, indeed, had come with him from 'Sumter': specifically Kell, first officer, Armstrong and Joe Wilson, second and third officers, both promoted from midshipman. John Low, fourth officer, had come out in 'Agrippina'. He, unusually, was from the Royal Naval Reserve, though had originally been born in Georgia. Arthur Sinclair, a young and relatively inexperienced man, was to be fifth officer. To these men Semmes confided his anxiety, then asked them to impress the sailors by wearing their brand new Confederate uniforms.

Semmes faced the parade. Without further ado the British flag was hauled down. A single cannon shot boomed. Semmes declared that from 24th August 1862 this ship was no longer Laird's 290, but 'Alabama' of the Confederate States Navy. A further shot was fired, and the Confederate colours were raised. A spontaneous cheer went up.

The captain next dropped his formal pose, leaped on to a higher position, and began an open appeal for enlistment, timing well the balance of his sailors' reason and emotion. He offered service with the 'Alabama', regular service for as long as she was afloat, or for the war's duration. Their uniform (interestingly, most sailors were attracted by this prospect) would be of finest blue and white, from a generous South, which now offered wages doubled from their previous earnings. Even more to the point, a substantial share of the anticipated money for bonded prizes would be granted, plus a bonus for each ship sunk. Their normal, everyday wants would be taken care of, including a high quality of rations and two tots of rum a day. With all this they would share in the glory to come. Semmes had finished, waved his hat toward paymaster Yonge, and invited all to join his ship.

The men split up into groups to argue. Some broke off to haggle with the paymaster, then returned to their colleagues. As the officers watched tensely, there was undoubtedly some hesitation. Then, suddenly one man strode forward to place his name on the wating papers. That settled it. A line formed, and soon 85 men had committed themselves to Confederate service. 'Alabama' had a crew. What a different outcome there had been on 'Florida'.

Next morning 'Bahama' left for England, carrying all those who had not signed on, while 'Agrippina' sailed westwards as coal and supply depot for the cruiser, bound eventually for their further rendezvous in November.

There was much to do on 'Alabama', not least training the men for war – how to use small arms, how to repel boarders, even how to tie knots. Thus several days passed, as the ship headed north in calm waters. Semmes' plan was to remain near the Azores and to intercept the regular whaling fleet from New England, expected at any time. Afterwards they would cruise toward the north-west, hoping to meet the eastbound grain fleets in the area of the Newfoundland Banks.

The wind began to get up. An Atlantic gale blew in on 'Alabama', making her roll heavily. All of a sudden, certain stowaways appeared from the boats, boys who had hidden themselves – presumably since Liverpool. After the initial surprise, Semmes was happy to sign them on the crew !

By the end of August 'Alabama' had already followed two sails, losing one in a long stern chase, but bringing to, at second try, a Portuguese brig, whose captain was somewhat taken aback at being accosted by a French warship, that day's disguise. The gale sank down to a breeze, and they cruised on, always between the Azores and the direction from which whalers might come. On September 2nd their policy paid off.

The 'Ocmulgee' was lying still, her sails furled, while the crew worked below on a recently captured sperm whale. Up swept 'Alabama', her Confederate colours now flying. The American sailors offered no resistance, since they knew nothing about Confederate raiders, and were more curious than resentful. Mindful of other whalers being sighted, Semmes decided only to put a prize crew aboard and took his 36 prisoners into 'Alabama'. But nothing more was seen that day.

In the morning, however, he decided to burn his prize after transferring provisions, rigging and other useful articles. Hoping that smoke would not frighten away any other ships, he used a firing technique learned on 'Sumter': all bunks and furniture were chopped up, then piled in the rooms affected. To the piles were added straw from mattresses and a liberal coating of lard or butter; a fuse led to the ship's side. The last men off lit the fuse, and leapt for their dingy. The 'Ocmulgee' already had some whale oil cargo, so she burned furiously and swiftly, masts crashing inward, ropes, wood and metal falling together in a fiery mass and slowly sinking.

On the 7th of September 'Alabama' was back in sight of Flores: the opportunity was taken to put their prisoners ashore. Incidentally, this was not quite the hardship it might seem, either for prisoners or for the local community. Semmes allowed each man released, a share in the booty captured, so that they went ashore richer than when on board – good for business on Flores. In fact, while 'Alabama' stayed in the vicinity, there was always a plentiful supply of booty, sailors and visitors coming into the local market. At that time the Confederates were popular in the Azores.

Soon another sail was sighted. This was no whaler, but a small American schooner, the 'Starlight', running westward, close inshore, an interesting problem for 'Alabama'. Semmes caught up with her, then showed his Confederate flag. At once the schooner swung landward. It was a critical moment, because both ships must have been close to the three mile limit, and the schooner was travelling fast. In desperation Semmes ordered off one warning shot, with no real expectation of stopping her. Yet that is what happened. Then a group of young girls crowded the side of their sailing vessel, and everyone knew why the 'Starlight' had given up. Undoubtedly, as Captain Semmes later admitted, they were right to surrender in the circumstances, but without women aboard, could easily have escaped.

'Starlight' was held near during the night, for the same reason as with 'Ocmulgee', but in the morning the ships reached Santa Cruz, a convenient place to put all prisoners ashore. The work was done quietly and efficiently, but so respectable did the Confederate crew seem in that port, that the governor of the island was induced to make an inspection of the 'Alabama', giving him the distinction of being the first colonial governor to step aboard a Confederate ship.

That same day the New England whaling fleet really began to arrive in the Azores, coming one by one in a way almost designed to suit 'Alabama'. Between 8th and 18th September the following were taken: 'Ocean Rover', 'Alert', 'Weather Gauge', 'Altamaha', 'Benjamin Tucker', 'Courser', 'Virginia' and 'Elisha Dunbar'. All were burnt, including the luckless 'Starlight', and excepting 'Courser', which was used as target practice for the Confederate gunners.

There was always a problem that smoke from the fires would give away the presence of 'Alabama', so Semmes tried scuttling one of the whalers instead. But he soon resolved never to repeat the experiment. As the whaler settled in the water, oil barrels came floating to the surface, to spread all over the sea. These were far more likely to give away his position. At the time they were not far from Flores, and enterprising locals appeared to pick up the fair gift of whale oil.

The Confederates could never understand why the whalers gave up so easily – after all they had no women on board – and even though the weather was fairly rough, making it difficult to aim the guns, one shot across the bows had generally sufficed. They might have tried to escape, with a fair chance of success, but didn't, and the whaling fleet had been destroyed.

The second phase for 'Alabama' was intended to be extinction of the New York to Europe grain fleet: and that to be accomplished as September's relative calm turned to the gales of October. 'Alabama' ploughed north-west into the weather, until she lay right across the grain route. Her luck held. There was no sign of the United States Navy as nine further captures were made and burned: the 'Emily Farnum', 'Brilliant', 'Wave Crest', 'Dunkirk', 'Tonawanda', 'Manchester', 'Lamplighter', 'Lafayette' and 'Crenshaw'. From the Confederates' point of view, on the other hand, there was perpetual discomfort, as they struggled to avoid collision with each grain ship in turn. It was necessary to row a small boat over to the prizes, a horrible duty, during which everyone experienced a ducking. It was fortunate, indeed, that no lives were lost, but there were many bruises and swallowings of salt water. A technique was developed to assist the boats, consisting of 'Alabama's driving to windward of the capture, loosing her boat to float with the wind, then moving to the lee side, so the small craft could again drift home more easily after finishing with the enemy. Much coal was used in these and other manoeuvres, fast emptying their bunkers.

One piece of eccentricity was Semmes' collection of chronometers, which accumulated as one came from each prize. Semmes insisted on bringing them to 'Alabama', after which each had to be wound regularly to avoid damage. That became the officer of the watch's duty, and because a winding took quite a lot of time, the routine became irksome. Sinclair expressed the view that if the current rate of hoarding was maintained, there would soon have to be an officer whose sole duty was winding.

Aboard the brigantine 'Dunkirk', bound for Lisbon, was found an old acquaintance of Semmes'. This was one George Forrest, deserter from the 'Sumter', now back in the merchant service. Forrest was at once tried by court martial, found guilty, and ordered to serve on 'Alabama' without pay or bonus money; a bad decision. He continued to cause trouble among the crew, and had eventually to be put ashore in the Caribbean.

In the middle of this success came 'Alabama's most trying time so far, for on the 17th of October the gale turned into a hurricane. At first 'Alabama' plunged wildly in the swell, carrying little sail. Then the mainyard split, broken in its slings, leaving no support for the ripping canvas of the main and maintopsails. Slashed to ribbons, they disappeared into the storm. The last tiny sail disintegrated in one terrifying moment. The wind drove so hard as to flatten the sea completely, while 'Alabama' heeled over until her gunports were under water, deck not quite awash.

It was in this situation that John Low, officer of the watch, made a crucial decision to "wear ship", without consulting the captain. He had suddenly felt the wind begin to change direction, with no slackening of pressure, and realised his decision must be immediate and correct, or the 'Alabama' would surely founder. So turn to face the weather he did, and so doing, created his own niche in the annals of the Confederate States Navy. 'Alabama' had been in the eye of the hurricane.

In the end the wind did fall. By 23rd October 'Alabama' was sailing through 'ordinary' rough sea, and her damage had been made good. That day, too, the 'Lafayette' was taken, and in spite of some argument about her ownership being British, went to the bottom. It was fortunate that Semmes was a lawyer, and could usually see through such arguments. 'Lafayette's captain insisted that, although originally American, she had been registered in Britain – as many had by this stage of the war. But he had no papers to prove it.

 'Alabama' ran south along the eastern seaboard of the United States. Semmes knew this could be a profitable course, though dangerous, and he half hoped to catch a Yankee troopship, taking reinforcements to one of the coastal outposts on the edge of the Confederacy. Another reason, of course, was that he had to rendezvous with 'Agrippina', and get some more coal supplies.

The last success in the grain fleet had been 'Crenshaw', and after that the barque 'Lauretta' fell just 200 miles from New York. It was all going so well. Papers captured along the way told them how 'Alabama' was generating confusion and uncertainty in the North and desperate efforts to catch her were being made. Yet no warships had been seen.

On 29th of October the brigantine 'Baron de Custine', carrying lumber from Cardenas, was bonded to take 45 more prisoners to safety. On the 2nd November another whaler, the 'Levi Starbuck', was intercepted, bringing fresh supplies and news. Thus matters continued. The newspapers, it seemed, were giving 'Alabama' a bad name, calling her a pirate, scavenger, and other less polite titles – a sure indication of Southern achievement.

Bermuda appeared in the distance, but there was no time to call. Instead they caught up with an India clipper, the 'T.B.Wales', with a cargo of linseed and saltpetre. She was burned. No troopships were sighted. After another quiet fortnight, Semmes dropped anchor in the calm waters of Fort de France bay, Martinique, just a year since he had been there in 'Sumter'. It was the 18th of November 1862, and, as promised, 'Agrippina' sailed up to 'Alabama' with her coal supply.

Local people remembered the good times with 'Sumter's sailors, so were quick to invite those from 'Alabama' to their clubs and inns – and to offer free liquor all round. Once ashore the storm-weary men of 'Alabama' really let themselves go, drunkenness developed into brawling, and on return to the ship became mutiny. Staggering dazedly about they cursed the officers and threw belaying pins at their imagined enemies. The ship's organisation was breaking down completely. Finally Semmes ordered a beat to quarters, and the men came into line. Thus was the mutiny quelled at the cost of some sore heads, while those still drunk were confined to the brig, to be sobered by cold water treatment. Foremost among the rabble had been George Forrest, still among the crew. He was ordered into the rigging and held there until the final decision was made to drop him at the next landfall.

The next problem was almost a repetition of the previous year's. As 'Alabama' lay in Fort de France, in sailed the 'San Jacinto', already made famous by the Mason and Slidell incident, but no longer commanded by Captain Wilkes. The French authorities reacted swiftly, again aware of the previous year's stand off and resolution, by giving notice of the 24 hour rule. 'San Jacinto' retreated to a safer station to watch 'Alabama', and a French gunboat placed herself between the two. The American captain quickly established a code of signals with agents ashore, while Semmes was advised by the French on how to make a clean getaway – quite a stance for a neutral. Both sides then waited.

There was indeed little hesitation. Semmes was certainly not afraid of 'San Jacinto': his ship had superior armament and speed. That very night he sailed straight out of harbour, and disappeared into the darkness. The crew of 'San Jacinto' failed to interpret or possibly even to see the frantic signals from their agents, and woke up to an empty Fort de France. Their opportunity was gone; not for many months afterwards would the United States have another.

'Alabama' rendezvoused with 'Agrippina', which had also left, near the desolate French Island of Blanquilla, some 300 miles away, off the coast of Venezuela. Here the coal transfer was to take place in peace.

The whole matter of supplying by coal ship was an interesting experiment. The Confederates had found that, in all other ports than British, enough coal was extremely hard to obtain, while the procedure called for much tact on the part of the cruiser captains. Sometimes, too, when a stock had been accumulated in advance by Confederate agents in those ports, it had been seized. Coal ships avoided time-wasting enquiries, gave some guarantee of supply availability, and kept the Confederates' presence secret. On the other hand, it was a disadvantage that meeting dates had to be kept, even if opportunities were lost as a result. Coaling at sea was inevitably slow, even in a calm bay. Each block of coal had to be carried by boat between the ships, or thrown by hand from deck to deck. On balance, a friendly reception in British ports remained their most convenient option.

At Blanquilla the Confederates were surprised to find a New England whaling schooner, the 'Clara L. Sparks', lying at anchor. She was not taken as a prize, being well inside French neutral waters, but was prevented from escaping to warn other ships. In the end, 'Clara L. Sparks' left in peace, without harassment.

On the 22nd of November coaling began in earnest, even continuing by night, with men working shifts. In between those, and away from repair duties, the sailors were free to wander on shore, to fish, or to amuse themselves in exploring the barren island. Blanquilla had a small population, indeed, there being but three goatherds, left to look after a few scrawny animals. Only a poor living could be extracted from the dry soil, so existence there must have been basic, and its value as a French colony very low. However, the sailors were able to catch some turtles, which the cook converted to edible meat. Blanquilla was made the dropping off point at last for George Forrest. No doubt until relief arrived, his would be a miserable existence.

Semmes' ambition now was to catch one of the clippers or steamships with gold from California. Since 1849 and the Gold Rush many cargoes of extraordinary wealth had rounded the Horn on their way to New York, passing to the east of the Indies. 'Alabama' was pushed out into their path; a keen watch kept. Petty Officer Evans, who had proven adept at spotting ships in the distance, was kept busy in the rigging. For a change they had a spell of fine weather, allowing the ship to be cleaned and polished, and nothing save the odd neutral vessel was seen, passing on an opposing track. On the 30th of November, however, there was excitement when the barque 'Parker Cook', of Boston, was found – but no gold. Instead it brought fresh pork, vegetables and other delicacies to the mess table. The prize was burned.

On the 5th of December they intercepted a Baltimore schooner, the 'Nina', on her way west with a British cargo. For that reason, and to relieve himself of the prisoners from 'Parker Cook', Semmes bonded 'Nina' for $15,000 and released her. This, in fact, represented a new policy for Maryland ships, which had previously been left alone. Based on recent Confederate failures in Maryland itself, as seen from captured newspapers, that state could now be regarded as hostile.

The two prizes acquired during the wait for a gold ship were regarded as poor compensation, but Semmes derived great satisfaction from newspapers aboard them. One article in the Baltimore Sun read:

"The shipments of grain from this port (Baltimore) during the past week have been almost entirely in foreign bottoms, the American flag being for the moment in disfavour, in consequence of the raid of the rebel steamer 'Alabama'.""

Even more illuminating was a letter in a New York paper:

"The damaging of the 'Alabama's raid on our shipping upon the maritime interests of this port were as conspicuous today as yesterday. It was next to impossible for the owner of a United States ship to procure freight unless he consented to make a bogus sale of his ship."

It was the last part of the letter that held Semmes' attention. He would be on his guard for 'bogus sales' from that day on, and it would take a sharp lawyer to find the difference between these and genuine sales. In the meantime concentrate on gold.

They hadn't long to wait. On the 6th December, a steam ship appeared from the north, travelling fast. The huge walking beam of her rear paddle wheel was plainly visible and she was immediately identifiable as one of the gold ships, the 'Ariel', albeit going the wrong way – empty. 'Alabama' moved toward her, crew at action stations, but with the United States flag disguise. Indeed, passengers lining the decks on 'Ariel' did think they were being approached by a US Navy gunboat. Then it was up with Confederate colours and off with a warning shot. Black smoke poured from their funnel, no attention was paid to 'Alabama's hail. Another shot, this time breaking splinters from the funnel, gave further notice. 'Ariel' came to a halt.

Semmes was very satisfied with his prize, because 'Ariel' belonged to the Vanderbilt Line, bitter enemies of the South before the war. Aboard were large quantities of guns and ammunition for transfer, but also a complete company of marines bound for California. Among the passengers mentioned above were a number of young women, whose obvious fear of the Confederates was based on the assumption of 'Alabama's piracy. Semmes sent his most handsome officers and crew in their best uniforms to quieten such doubts, and so successful were they, that the girls were soon drinking toasts to President Davis. In return Lt. Armstrong wished good health to President Lincoln and all Northern politicians – and was relieved of his dress buttons as souvenirs of the day !

'Ariel' was held alongside as they waited a while longer. A gold ship was due – the crew of 'Ariel' confirmed that – but nothing seen.(In fact, the California steamer 'Champion' had passed them, going north, but over the horizon). It was all very frustrating, and never was a good idea for 'Alabama' to remain long in one place. Semmes decided to take his prisoners into Jamaica, then to sink 'Ariel'.

Events, however, ruined this plan, even as they sailed west, when yet another ship appeared, on a course out of Jamaica. 'Alabama' gave chase, but was almost immediately immobilised by engine trouble. Now that meant trouble, because repairs at sea could take days, and 'Alabama' would be in no position to stop 'Ariel' escaping. Instead, Semmes despatched his whaleboat to stop the newcomer, calculating correctly that the lightness of the breeze would hold her back.

Though it was an anticlimax to discover that the unidentified stranger was a German brig, it was nothing to the other news which greeted 'Alabama's boarding party. The German had left Kingston, Jamaica that very day, and reported the presence of rampant yellow fever there. Kingston was the only acceptable port available, so Semmes had again to change plans. He bonded 'Ariel' for $261,000, a sum never exceeded in the war, and sent her on her way with crew and prisoners. The party of marines were sworn not to bear arms against the Confederacy for the duration of the war, but there was, in any case, little animosity. The passengers and crews had rather enjoyed their time together.

The engine repairs on 'Alabama' did take fully three days, leaving Semmes impatient and fretting: nothing he could do except wait. Afterwards it was almost time for their next rendezvous with 'Agrippina' off the Mexican coast, so in that direction they must sail. To cap it, the weather turned nasty again from the north, and heavy seas threw them toward the northern shore of Jamaica. Nevertheless, 'Alabama' rounded Cape Catouche in Yucatan by the 20th December, and, crossing the Gulf of Campeche, met 'Agrippina' in the Arca Islands on the 23rd. Both ships anchored to the south of one of the islands, protected from storms.

The Arcas are barren islands, home only to thousands of seabirds, but are surrounded by coral reef. Inside the reef, therefore, the water was calm, while everything below sea level was clear and colourful: a good place for the rest Semmes and his crew needed. It was Christmas 1862, 'Alabama' had 26 prizes to show for her cruise so far, and that could be counted as success.

In the United States the reputation of 'Alabama' already overshadowed anything else done by the Confederates at sea, and they had no idea where she was.

CHAPTER SIX

The Caribbean & the Gulf of Mexico, January 1863

At the end of 1862 the American Civil War was finely balanced. Both sides had hoped for a quick victory, though neither had achieved it: and no end was in sight.

However, the Confederacy was faced with a continuing and now effective blockade of its ports, and many of the ships trying to break through were being caught. That didn't help – the South simply had to import the means to make war, or it would eventually lose. Thus, the blockade had to be defeated, a difficult prospect, or the United States warships guarding the Southern coast had to be drawn off – and that is where 'Florida' and 'Alabama' were so important.

There was some reason for Southern optimism over the cruisers. By their earlier efforts 'Sumter' and 'Alabama' had caused disruption in the Atlantic and around the West Indies, and no-one knew where 'Alabama' would appear next. 'Florida' in Mobile was also a potential threat, even if she had been unsuccessful so far.

For many months, in fact, the United States government had given plenty of attention to the problem, at first supporting, but eventually disagreeing with the naval policy of putting the blockade first. Secretary-of-the-Navy Gideon Welles had effectively allowed the depredations of the rebel cruisers, as not too high a price to pay for stationing all available warships, especially the newer ones, around the Southern coast. Few had been sent out to protect their merchant fleet.

However, by the end of 1862 popular pressure was building against him. The long casualty list of prizes taken – 'Alabama' alone, 26 ships taken in 1862 - was seen by the North against the apparent incompetence of their navy. In 1861 U.S.S. 'Tuscarora' had failed to stop the 'Nashville', in 1862 had been helpless at the escape of 'Oreto' and 290 from Britain, while three ships had been unable to catch 'Sumter'. Humiliation followed as 'Florida' and 'Alabama' were easily able to outrun and outguess 'Onward',

'St. Louis' and 'Kearsage' across the Atlantic. Worst of all had the failure to stop 'Florida' as she swept into Mobile. The President called for some better ideas.

A fresh policy had to be possible, and once Welles turned his mind to it, he came up with a three point proposal – which still left his blockade in place.

First, a squadron of warships should be based permanently in the West Indies, to close that area completely.

Second, powerful ships should be fitted out with the single purpose of hunting down the rebel raiders.

Third, owing to shortage of naval vessels the use of letter of marque privateers should be considered.

This third suggestion was unpopular. Coupled with the sense of guilt over using weapons for which they had condemned the rebels, was an anxiety that such privateers might get out of hand, and being tempted by richer targets than the 'Alabama', might sink into straightforward piracy. The privateer clause was dropped.

President Lincoln, however, approved of the West Indies fleet, and acted decisively with the appointment of Charles Wilkes, popular hero of the Mason and Slidell affair. In January 1863 Wilkes was promoted to admiral, given the 'Wachusett', 'Dacotah', 'Cimmaron', 'Sonoma', 'Tioga', 'Octorora' and 'Santiaga de Cuba', all sloops or gunboats, and sent to the Danish island of St.Thomas in the Virgin Islands where the United States maintained a base, his task to eliminate those tiresome Confederate cruisers.

From the beginning Wilkes concerned himself with the British, in the knowledge that nearly all the arms, medicines and other war supplies running into Southern ports were under British flag. The fleet moved to Bermuda, demanding word of 'Alabama', and finding none, left 'Sonoma' on guard there, almost as a blockade. The idea was to prevent all craft which might be blockade runners from leaving harbour until they had been inspected and cleared. Of course, the presence of 'Sonoma' soon provoked a row between governments.

Next Wilkes descended upon Nassau, chased the British about, and attempted to close down the Britain-West Indies trade. Later again he arrived at Barbados, and accused the resident governor of offering hospitality to Confederate sailors – tactless, if probably true. Wilkes was becoming an embarrassment to his government.

His worst action, however, and one that made him very unpopular in Washington, was the retention of 'Vanderbilt'. Welles' second recommendation had been accepted, and a brand new ship capable of outrunning and outgunning 'Alabama' had been built. Called the 'Vanderbilt', it was sent out in February 1863 with 'Alabama' in mind. Unfortunately, a course was set right through the West Indies, through

Wilkes' area of responsibility, and the admiral at once took a liking to her. Overbearing her captain by rank, Wilkes moved his flag to 'Vanderbilt', and there it stayed for some months. By the time an increasingly desperate War Department managed to wrest 'Vanderbilt' from the West Indies fleet, the 'Alabama' had left the Gulf and was well ahead of any pursuit. At the least, one chance to catch her had been lost.

Apart from the British, however, the first problem for Charles Wilkes in 1863 was another cruiser, the 'Retribution'. She was a schooner, captured at the beginning of the war in Wilmington, North Carolina, and probably the last letter of marque privateer to be commissioned by the Confederates. 'Retribution' ran the blockade on 7th December 1862, and having disposed of her cargo of cotton at a British colonial port, moved to the Venezuelan coast for a secret rendezvous. Her Captain Parker had arranged that a Danish steamer with guns and ammunition (from St. Thomas ?) would be there, and transfer was soon made. It seems that Parker now sailed into the neutral port of St. Thomas (the capital of the island of St. Thomas, and not that American base mentioned above). There he discovered merchant ships in the harbour, saved by neutrality from attack. A boat was, however, rowed across to the 'Gilmore Meredith', an American ship, and five men were persuaded to switch sides. Finally 'Retribution' slipped away into the maze of islands thereabouts, to become a hot subject of rumour, and to be a prime target for Wilkes' new command.

It appears that on about the 10th of January 1863 Parker came upon the steamer 'J.P.Ellicott', a Maine vessel bound for Cienfuegos, on her route near Haiti. Made a prize, she was ordered to a Confederate port with her crew as prisoners. Unfortunately, the latter managed to escape and overcame their captors, so no profits were gained for the South.

Next, 'Retribution' appeared in the Bahamas, escorting a new prize, the Boston sailing ship 'Hanover'. Parker now seems to have ignored the rules of neutrality, for he shipped his prize right into Nassau, this a breach in itself, and sold the cargo for his own gain. Unwilling to lose an opportunity, he loaded 'Hanover' with a further cargo of salt, and despatched her to Wilmington – which harbour was eventually reached.

A third capture locally was the brig 'Emily Fisher', but, as this was not taken until the 19th of February, 'Retribution' must have been in or around the Bahamas and free from pursuit for a whole month. Perhaps Wilkes' ships were too busy with the other cruisers – more of them below – but the ease with which 'Retribution' operated did nothing for his reputation.

In the end 'Retribution' was overtaken by the strain of her journey. She had not been a new ship at the start, indeed, had been in poor condition then, and it took only a few months continuous sailing to render her unseaworthy. Parker decided to take his ship into Nassau again, and there sold her profitably. His cruise had certainly been worth while financially and of good service to the Confederacy.

His own destiny was rather less outstanding, because Captain Parker next contrived a plan to capture a ship for himself. Leaving Nassau behind, he booked into a vessel bound for St. John's, Nova Scotia. Once there, he took passage on an American steamer, the 'Chesapeake', and carried out his plot to overthrow the officers and crew. The plot failed, although Parker himself managed to escape by swimming ashore – just as well, too; he thought of himself as a Confederate sailor, but in fact was just a common felon, and could rightly have been accused of piracy.

The voyage of 'Retribution' had depressed those hoping the West Indies fleet would be victorious. But that was nothing to the fresh exploits of 'Alabama' and 'Florida'. At the beginning of 1863 no one in the United States knew where 'Alabama' was, except that she had been seen near Jamaica, and was obviously not far away. Hopefully Captain Wilkes would find her.

'Alabama' though, left the Arcas Islands after Christmas, and by the early days of January was steaming rapidly north, unmolested, and set upon a freshly considered plan. Semmes had the port of Galveston in mind, because reports reaching him via his various captures mentioned a combined naval and military expeditionary force heading that way. Many potential prizes would be present, and nobody would expect a Confederate cruiser to appear. Semmes proposed to sail right into the assembled shipping, to scatter, sink or burn as many transports as came into his power, thus hopefully ruining the whole campaign.

On the 15th of January 'Alabama' approached Galveston, and at noon was about thirty miles away, out of sight of the very flat shoreline. Semmes cut speed, for he intended to hold off until the next morning – when twelve hours of daylight would be available. From thirty miles away there was no sign of the flat, featureless coast, and nothing to see except a few topsails grouped together, scarcely moving. Were they just the Galveston blockade ? In vain Semmes looked about for the expected armada of transports. Instead he suddenly noticed one of the sails turning, a vessel apparently heading his way – that had to be a blockader, and their approach had been seen.

Everyone on 'Alabama' knew she could be a match for an individual Union warship, so Semmes needed little encouragement. By sailing slowly away from Galveston, he would convince his enemy that his own course was of a discrete and normal blockade runner, while ensuring the battle would take place far away from any help: and so it turned out. The U.S.S. 'Hatteras', a paddle steamer and ex-river boat, came up rapidly, fully expecting to capture yet another blockade runner, and Captain Blake hailed the stranger. 'Alabama' was flying her British flag at this stage.

"What ship is that ?"

"This is H.M.S. 'Vixen'". The two ships were barely 75 yards apart.

"We're lowering a boat to go alongside you"- then suddenly came a different call.

"We are the Confederate States steamer 'Alabama'". At once a new flag whipped out, while gunports swung open, and before anyone could answer, a paralysing volley of shot splintered the side of 'Hatteras'. Desperately Blake closed the 'Alabama' and opened fire himself, but found his ship too slow to avoid fire from the depressed guns. Quickly, holes were broken at waterline and below deck. 'Hatteras' listed hard to port, lost her port battery overside, and began to settle. Blake had no choice but to surrender.

'Hatteras' sank bow first, leaving only a stream of air bubbles. The fight had lasted merely fifteen minutes.

When every survivor had been collected, the 'Alabama' got up steam and headed south with her prisoners, away from Galveston, back into the obscurity she relied on.

When more United States vessels finally arrived to help out, they found only the masts of 'Hatteras' protruding above the water. The Gulf is very shallow in places, especially near the coast. Amazingly, her flag was still flying above the sea.

However, the fight remained no mystery. The rowing boat, originally set down to board 'Alabama', had survived, and those sailors escaped to reach the shore. They told of Confederate treachery in pretending to be British, yet also of Confederate honour, in picking up every swimming seaman. They could describe the great fire power of their enemy. They could not know, however, that, in spite of all, only two men aboard 'Hatteras' had been killed and seven wounded, while the carpenter on 'Alabama' was her sole casualty, and he but slightly hurt. Nor could they report that 'Alabama' had, indeed, been hit by their gunfire, albeit in just a few non-vital places.

Comparative Armaments: (poundage refers to weight of solid shot fired – thus a 32 pounder fires shot of weight 32 pounds. Shells are explosive, rather than solid shot)

C.S.S.'Alabama' :	6 long 32 pounders	192 lbs
	1 rifled 100 pounder	100 lbs
	1 eight inch shell gun	68 lbs
	Total	360 lbs
U.S.S. 'Hatteras' :	4 short 32 pounders	128 lbs
	2 rifled 30 pounders	60 lbs
	1 rifled 20 pounder	20 lbs
	1 howitzer	12 lbs
	Total	220 lbs

The 'Hatteras' episode certainly caused an outcry in the North. The Confederates had sunk a warship in naval combat, and still the 'Alabama' remained loose. Would she now try to break out into the Atlantic Ocean ? The West Indies squadron was ordered to be alert. Yet there was more trouble to come, because 'Florida' was set to escape from Mobile.

After she had broken into the heavily blockaded port, 'Florida' had been in dock or at anchor for several months. The yellow fever had finally disappeared, its last unfortunate victim being the heroic John Stribling. Work had thereafter gone ahead on repairs. Much had also been done to establish a full crew, for there were many unemployed sailors in Mobile, while James Maffit was back in good health. By the beginning of 1863 'Florida' was ready.

Now it was necessary to choose the correct weather – preferably stormy – to give their passage through the blockade the best chance. At least seven ships were on duty outside, including the U.S.S 'Cuyler', 'Susquehanna' and 'Oneida', all as fast as 'Florida' and more heavily armed. Maffit waited his moment, in spite of pressure from some ashore to get going. On the 15th of January it was a grey morning, with a fine drizzle in the air, and he steamed down the bay to wait for darkness under the guns of Fort Morgan. Then came the weather change Maffit wanted, a steadily rising wind blowing the gloom away, and he was away.

By the time 'Florida' came into the open, any mistiness had been replaced by stormy conditions, visibility now spoiled by spray and heavy seas. 'Florida' steamed right between the blockading ships, passed but 300 yards from 'Cuyler' before the crew of that vessel realised the danger.

When the blockaders did eventually get under way, they were too late. By morning 'Florida' was still in sight, though far ahead. By the evening of the 16th January she had disappeared into the Gulf.

This failure was worse for the North than the sinking of 'Hatteras'. At least with the latter there was the apparent mitigation of treachery, and a fight had taken place. 'Florida' had provided no such comfort, not even in the chase, and plainly the navy might have done better. Until the sinking of 'Alabama' in 1864, some stigma of their inferiority would remain.

In late January 'Alabama' and 'Florida' were both loose, most likely heading for an escape into the Atlantic, after which plenty of trouble for American commerce could be expected. Could Charles Wilkes and the recently set up West Indies squadron prevent that happening ?

As mentioned above, Wilkes' first move in January was to investigate Bermuda, his second, Nassau in the Bahamas, and his third to find the 'Retribution'. He wasn't covering either the Yucatan Passage or the Florida Straits, the only ways out of the Gulf of Mexico. He therefore missed 'Florida' completely, because she went straight from Mobile through the northern passage via Havana to Nassau, picking up her first three prizes en route. That journey took only a few days. In Nassau Maffit was agreeably surprised by the immediate offer of three months coal supply – embarrassing when compared to the minimum being granted to United States ships. However, it suited the Confederates, because Maffit was anxious to be on and away from the islands. U,S,S. 'Sonoma' was reported to be somewhere nearby. As it happened, Charles Wilkes was still making the wrong decisions, having heard that 'Florida' had coaled in Nassau. He assumed another coaling before the Atlantic would be necessary, but that in accordance with neutrality laws, no British colony would dare to fuel 'Florida' within the month. Wilkes therefore concentrated his fleet on French Martinique, well to the south, where Maffit might just have to go: and yet he was wrong. Maffit was able to pick up 100 tons of coal in Barbados, capturing another prize on the way. From there 'Florida' was off into the Atlantic by early February, beyond the range of the West Indies squadron. Wilkes found himself in time only to detain two pursuers from Mobile, 'Oneida' and 'Cuyler' of the blockading force, compelling them both to become part of his own fleet. Even that was before the checking of 'Vanderbilt', discussed earlier.

Wilkes did have a better opportunity to find 'Alabama'. She had sailed away with her prisoners from the battle off Galveston, but by the 20th of January was still accessible in Port Royal, Jamaica, obviously in no hurry to move on. Jamaica was then, of course, a British possession, so the Confederates received their customary excited welcome. Port Royal harbour, in fact, was full of British warships, whose crews were most enthusiastic to see 'Alabama'. On H.M.S. 'Greyhound' a marine band thought it fitting to play Dixie as a signal of approval – only much later balancing their programme by playing Yankee Doodle Dandy.

The real attraction in Jamaica, though, was rum. As boats ferrying both 'Alabama's crew and prisoners from 'Hatteras' reached shore, a concerted rush to the local inns took place, and Union and Confederate sailors drank deeply together in the greatest friendship. The inns did very good business, storing up some trouble for the sailors' return.

As it happened, Captain Semmes had taken the opportunity of visiting friends inland, leaving his ship in the hands of Lt. Kell. This officer was now faced with drunken seamen – initially two who, being arrested on the dock, jumped overboard after their return, and seized a passing rowing boat. Ejecting the occupants, they tried to escape back into Port Royal, and only failed from alcoholic exhaustion.

More seriously, Kell was obliged to detain paymaster Yonge for working against the interests of his ship. Yonge had never been a great favourite on board, for his habits of fraternising and drinking with the crew had sometimes been an embarrassment to his fellow officers. It was in Jamaica, however, that he brought trouble to 'Alabama' by being continually drunk and siding with the lower decks against the officers.

In the course of such disputes, he was seen talking to the United States consul, and soon his influence was causing men to change sides. Kell couldn't tolerate treason, and arrested Yonge immediately.

When Semmes found what had happened, he had no hesitation in removing the paymaster from 'Alabama' for good. The officer was dismissed from Confederate service: and that was the end of a very disagreeable matter. (Incidentally, Yonge turned up in England after the war to testify against his old vessel in the course of the 'Alabama' claims).

After five days the fun was over, the ship fully provisioned and fuelled for the next stage of their cruise. All hands being persuaded to work again, Semmes put to sea, still having seen no sign of a Union warship. Indeed, 'Alabama' would remain in the West Indies for another week, almost waiting to be challenged. But nothing untoward happened.

A poem commemorating the escape of 'Florida' from Mobile was written later by a member of her crew:

Cruise of the 'Florida'

Nine cruisers they had, and they lay off the bar
Their long line to seaward extending so far;
And Preble, he said, as he shut his eyes tight:
"I'm sure they're all hammocked this cold bitter night."

Bold Maffitt commanded, a man of great fame,
He sailed in the Dolphin – you've heard of the same;
He called us all aft, and these words did he say:
"I'm bound to run out, boys; up anchor, away !"

Our hull was well whitewashed, our sails were all stowed,
Our steam was chock up, and the fresh wind it blowed:
As we crawled along by them, the yanks gave a shout –
We dropped all our canvas, and opened her out.

You'd have thought them all mad if you'd heard the cursed racket
They made upon seeing our flash little packet;
Their boatswains did pipe, and the blue light did play,
And the great Drummond light, it turned night into day.

The 'Cuyler', a boat that's unrivalled for speed,
Quick let slip her cables, and quickly indeed,
She thought for to catch us, and keep us in play,
Till her larger companions could get under way.

She chased and she chased till at dawning of day
From her backers she thought she was too far away;
So she gave up the chase, and reported, no doubt,
That she'd sunk us and burned us – somewhere thereabout.

So when we were out, boys, all on the salt sea,
We brought the 'Estelle' to, right under our lee,
And burned her and sunk her, with all her fine gear,
And sailed straight for Havana, the bold privateer.

Huzza ! Huzza ! For the 'Florida's crew.
We'll range with bold Maffitt the world through and through.

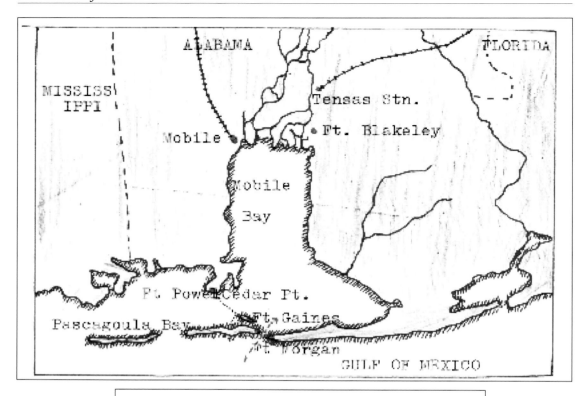

MOBILE & ENVIRONS

------ *Channel for blockade runners*   .... *Boom Defences*

CHAPTER SEVEN

Disorder in the Atlantic

From the 25th of January 1863 'Alabama' lingered a full week in West Indian waters. Indeed, Semmes never moved far from the larger islands, hoping to intercept some short distance traffic. Two ships were captured, both with valuable cargo, and both were burned. The 'Golden Rule' actually carried a certificate of neutrality, but Semmes was able to use his legal training to refute that claim, and his prize joined 'Chastelaine' on the seabed.

However, with American ships growing wary of the Caribbean, there wasn't much work for the Confederates. They would have to move on, because even Wilkes would find 'Alabama' in the end. Accordingly, Semmes dropped prisoners in San Domingo, then headed north for the open sea, intending to make a wide sweep into the Atlantic before turning south for the Brazilian coast.

In fact this course brought about one of the most fruitful episodes of their cruise, embracing the main East Indies, India, Pacific and San Roque trade routes. By steering north-east up to the 30th parallel, Semmes would place 'Alabama' squarely between New York and the homeward bound freighters. It would be relatively easy to sail slowly along this track, picking up prizes as they passed. Eventually they would arrive in the vicinity of the equator, nearly approaching the eastern tip of Brazil – the crossroads of the Atlantic - where all ships must pass through a channel barely 60 miles wide, the only route to the north for many miles east of South America. There would inevitably be a great concentration of shipping, but equally so, there might be enemy warships waiting. (Indeed, the 'Vanderbilt', specifically designed to take on the 'Alabama', would have turned up if Wilkes had not prevented it).

Soon after leaving San Domingo 'Alabama's crew experienced the frights of a fire at sea. Nothing more terrifying could happen, for against a serious blaze they could do little. However, the reported fire was small, a petty officer having carried a lighted candle into the alcohol store, where some of the inflammable vapour was well diffused into the atmosphere. It was quickly brought under control, much to the relief of all, but Semmes could not allow the offence to pass. He promptly demoted the petty officer.

Next day 'Alabama' found and burned the schooner 'Palmetto'. The Confederates pressed on, hopeful of success on the northern leg of their cruise. Yet a full fortnight now passed without any sightings, until on the 21st of February four American ships appeared together, though separating rapidly at her approach. Semmes ordered more steam from the boilers, got it, and sped toward the nearest and slowest vessel. Two shots into her rigging convinced the captain of 'Golden Eagle' of his hopeless position, and, as soon as a prize crew had boarded her, Semmes rushed off for another ship still visible in the distance. The 'Olive Jane', caught after a two hour chase, proved to be a well-stocked provision ship, and furnished 'Alabama's crew with luxuries normally unseen. After a considerable looting, this prize was sunk, while Semmes turned back to deal with his earlier capture.

In the next few days, astride the main commerce route, 'Alabama' accounted for three more American merchantmen, though kept even more busy checking the papers of ostensible neutrals. Many of those had to be suspect, of course, even though they appeared to be legitimate. Shippers were gradually learning how to counter the Confederates.

One of the three taken was bonded for $50,000, in order to carry off the many prisoners on 'Alabama' – just as well, because things were getting uncomfortable below, and they were about to enter a period of gales on their way south. The Confederates would have been seriously hampered. As it was, the crew of another prize, the barque 'John A. Parks', taken just after the bonded vessel left, were caught in the worsening weather. It was lucky that a friendly British ship passed by and took off the new prisoners.

By the 12th of March 'Alabama' was only 12 degrees from the equator, bucking and rolling wildly through a strangely cold ocean. It was slow work, with horizontal rain in their faces, almost a reminder of the experiences near Newfoundland. However, the further south they got, the more they expected to see ships from the Brazilian coast bottleneck – on the 14th the 'Punjaub', a Boston ship carrying linseed for London, was stopped. Because her cargo was British, Semmes decided only on bonding, and sent 'Punjaub' on her way.

Another four merchantmen were captured between 23rd and 24th of March, one again being bonded for prisoner removal, the other three burned. Then, by a real stroke of luck, on the 4th of April a coal ship, 'Louisa Hatch', fell into their hands, just as the bad weather began to relent and just as refuelling was becoming due. Semmes was expecting

'Agrippina' very shortly with a fresh load of Welsh coal, but still had in his mind the inevitable uncertainty of their rendezvous. If 'Agrippina' failed to show up, he could help himself from 'Louisa Hatch'. For the moment, therefore, that prize was retained to sail with 'Alabama'.

Fernando de Noronha is the largest of a small group of islands about one hundred and fifty miles from the eastern coast of Brazil. Being volcanic in origin, the islands are mountainous and rocky, yet well wooded, with much good land for agriculture on the lower slopes. The islands were Spanish property at the time, and were used as a penal settlement – even the governor was a convict, trusted with control over the thousand or so inhabitants. Fernando was the planned meeting point for coaling.

For some time, however, Semmes couldn't even find it himself. As the turbulent seas became calm, fog and heavy rain reduced visibility to a frustrating minimum. No land was seen, and Semmes even tried taking coal from 'Louisa Hatch' in the open sea – not a good idea; very slow and with a great danger of capsizing an overloaded rowing boat. Coaling at sea was soon abandoned.

In the end, of course, their navigation was proven correct. After a week of searching they did finally arrive in the bay of Fernando de Noronha, much to everyone's relief – but no 'Agrippina' was in sight. Semmes would have to wait, coaling slowly in the meantime from 'Louisa Hatch', while he made friends with the governor. (Semmes offered 'Louisa Hatch' to Spain, through the governor, for $20,000. The offer had to be refused, because, there was not so much money on the islands, but in compensation the Confederates were granted full rights for landing and reprovisioning).

Unknown to the fretting Semmes 'Agrippina' was at that moment hurrying toward the Spanish colony, having sailed from the Arcas to Cardiff, there to load 'the finest coal available when Pennsylvania anthracite was not'. She was very late coming back, though, and her Captain McQueen was well aware of it. No effort to catch up was being spared.

As rain dripped monotonously down on April 14th, alarm signals rang again. Two ships had been sighted, both flying United States colours, sailing fast into the bay. At once someone hoisted the United States flag on 'Alabama' – this time they would pretend to be a navy warship. But the strangers were suspicious, lowering four small boats to inspect and study. That over and doubts satisfied, the four headed for shore, apparently to land their crews on the beach. Semmes' moment had now come, because all attention aboard the two American vessels was on their boats, and both, he noticed, were still outside the three mile limit. 'Alabama' was upon them immediately, and 'Lafayette' and 'Kate Cory' were boarded in the name of the Confederacy.

Semmes waited until the 22nd of April for 'Agrippina', but, finally losing patience, decided he could stay no longer. From the social point of view, of course, Fernando de Noronha had been a great success, what with the friendly governor sending out fruit and turkeys to the Confederates, and altogether showing sympathy for their cause. On the other hand, Semmes had to get on – it was certainly dangerous to stay too long in one place. He left the four captured boats for local seamen to use, but burned and sank all his recent prizes, including 'Louisa Hatch'. 'Alabama' sailed directly for Bahia (now Salvador) on the Brazilian coast, arriving there on May 11th.

There remained disappointment at the failure of 'Agrippina', which led to a change of policy by Semmes. In future he would rely on his own powers of persuasion to obtain coal in port, and would scrap the whole idea of supply ships. As for 'Agrippina' herself, she did eventually arrive in Fernando, and finding 'Alabama' gone to Bahia, McQueen tried desperately to reach that port in time. Unfortunately, he was again too late, and being uncertain where to go next, hesitated in port for just a few days. A bad mistake: the United States warships 'Mohican' and 'Onward' (not from the West Indies squadron) made a sudden appearance at Bahia, and their blockade prevented 'Agrippina' from taking any further part.

A swifter use of Brazilian ports by the Confederates was, on the other hand a good idea. Not only was the coast close to main shipping lanes, but Brazil was an independent country recently free from European domination. There was thus an understanding of the South's position and much sympathy. Help might be expected – countered only at times by the influence of the United States Consulate. 'Alabama' was welcomed into Bahia, just as 'Sumter' had been in Maranham.

Imagine the excitement, too, when another Confederate ship arrived, for into Bahia on the 13th of May 1863 sailed the 'Georgia', fresh from Europe with her tender and coal ship, 'Castor'.

'Georgia' had started as 'Virginia', and, as mentioned in the chapter on Liverpool, had been part of James Bulloch's campaign in Britain. After his experiences with 'Florida' and 'Alabama', Bulloch had been wary of building ships in Liverpool, so in late 1862 'Virginia' was ordered from a yard in Dumbarton, on the Clyde, and was ostensibly stated to be for China. Interestingly, she didn't attract much hostile attention from the United States, probably because her design was of a normal merchant vessel, with none of the sleek appearance of her predecessors – certainly a disadvantage at sea, even if it helped to disguise her during construction. As a price for freedom 'Virginia' suffered loss of manoeuvrability, lack of speed, and an inability to ride easily on sail or steam alone. Steam had therefore to be kept in most of the time, while her coal bunkers were insufficient anyway to support a lengthy cruise. Refuelling would become a constant problem.

On the 27th of March 1863 'Virginia' was changed to 'Japan', then moved down river to Greenock, where a crew of 80 men was shipped. On the 30th she was registered in Liverpool, allowing her the privilege of flying a British flag, and so out to sea, before any suspicions were able to form. For provisioning and arming Bulloch employed his usual method, sending out the steamer 'Alar' from Newhaven, loaded with warlike material, and carrying Lieutenant Maury (son of the famous naval officer and oceanographer Matthew Maury) to take command. The two ships met off Ushant, and a complete transfer of cargo was effected in three days – very smart work, this, conducted in the open sea in difficult circumstances.

When all the work was done, the well-rehearsed scenes practised aboard earlier Confederate cruisers were repeated. Bewildered but half suspecting sailors were confronted with the sudden appearance of Lieutenant Maury in full Confederate uniform, backed by his new complement of young, fresh officers from the Southern Naval Academy. With the usual ceremony Maury saw the rebel flag hoisted, then heard his ship renamed 'Georgia' – all on the 10th of April 1863.

Maury had by his side an invaluable officer of the old 'Sumter'. Lieutenant John Evans had of course gained his experience under Raphael Semmes, and like him, appreciated the importance for European opinion, of removing the American Atlantic trade. Working with Maury, the plan was to make a wide sweep across that ocean, before moving south to the Brazilian coast. They would not cruise into the West Indies.

However, their plan reckoned without the effect of previous raiders. In fact, the Atlantic trade was a shadow of its former self, and few sails were seen during their crossing. Those that were, had no difficulty in outrunning 'Georgia', and it was now that her limitations became apparent. Maury decided to sail south, to look for slower victims clinging to the South American coastline – and with that purpose arrived in Bahia. What a boost to their sailors to see 'Alabama'. In 1863 it was a great thing to serve on a Confederate ship; and when two were together, it was truly a cause for celebration.

There was further good fortune for Semmes, because a tender and coaling ship, the 'Castor', had been ordered to rendezvous with 'Georgia' at Bahia. Her prompt arrival more than made up for the non-appearance of 'Agrippina'. Both cruisers were able to take on large stocks of fuel.

Less happy was the Brazilian government, for whom the presence of three Confederate ships and a vociferous United States consul was a little too much. Semmes and Maury were urged to leave as soon as possible.

As it happened both were indeed anxious not to waste time, especially with the always imminent threat of being caught by enemy warships. Their crews, too, were becoming a nuisance on shore. Because both captains wanted to go next to the Cape of Good Hope, where they would cross another trade route, it was agreed that 'Alabama' would leave first. 'Georgia' could follow in a few days, when coaling was complete. This ought to be a fair arrangement, because after leaving Bahia, little success was expected in the South Atlantic – until the north/south route along the African coast was reached. As both ships would cross that at different times, both could have good opportunities. From Capetown, 'Georgia' would turn north, while 'Alabama' was destined for the Indian Ocean. Their co-operation was therefore only for the immediate future.

Accordingly, the 24th of May saw 'Alabama's flag dipped to her friends, then her departure to the cheers of both companies of sailors.

It was hot and calm as they sailed south, but the seas were not immediately empty as expected. Two captures were made the next day, one burned, the other bonded, while yet a third was burned on the 26th after a five hour chase. Semmes resolved to stay close to South America for a bit longer, and was rewarded by a further five prizes up to the 4th of July. Most of them were burned after transfer of valuable provisions, but the 'Conrad' was deemed suitable for conversion to warship. More of her later.

'Alabama' did now head east for South Africa, seeing no more potential prizes, and finally reaching the coast at Saldanha Bay on the 29th of July. Surely a reprovisioning halt was due, an opportunity to fix those inevitable leaks, to apply some paint, and even perhaps to take a break on shore. Saldanha, though, seemed to have little attraction for the sailors; no busy and prosperous port, no entertainments; merely a gloomy inlet with a few houses, backed by bare tree-less hills and rough grass. Fine soil stained the sea a muddy brown: all in all, quite an unappealing view.

Once ashore, though, the Dutch-speaking inhabitants, mainly farmers, did their best to put on some fine hospitality, and showed great interest in 'Alabama'. Their hard life at Saldanha, they explained, was certainly tempered by the good shooting to be had locally. Pheasant were plentiful, as were other birds, rabbits and deer. Indeed, they would prove their words by inviting the Confederate officers to take part.

Unfortunately, it was that shooting which spoiled their visit to Saldanha. They could not foresee that Third Engineer Cummings would be so careless as to reload his musket with the gun pointing straight for him. He pulled the trigger by mistake, and died before anyone could reach the spot.

After they had buried Cummings, the general desire was to leave a place where 'Alabama's first casualty had been recorded. It was all the more disturbing because Engineer Cummings had not been killed in action, but had apparently thrown his life away for a pheasant. 'Alabama' sailed out of the bay, for morale to recover in the open sea. She was a good ship, after all, and the officers and crew were generally at ease with each other. A few hours of fine sunny weather and an issue of rum soon drove out the depression. 'Alabama' headed south.

Time here to report on that fresh Confederate raider, the converted 'Conrad', whose capture off South America had been in late May. She had a valuable cargo of wool, bound for New York, and no doubt that could be sold in the end – better than burning, in any event. She also looked a fast sailer. As it happened, another capture in June, shortly before 'Conrad', had yielded two 12 pound guns, and these were transferred. 'Conrad' was rechristened 'Tuscaloosa', placed under the command of 'Alabama's 4th Lieutenant Low, and sent off to cruise independently but roughly in parallel – the two captains agreed to meet again in Cape Town.

In fact, that meeting took place much earlier than intended, shortly after 'Alabama' left Saldanha Bay. Indeed, it would be fair to say that the latter captured her original prize again, because 'Tuscaloosa' was at first identified as a United States merchantman, and 'Alabama' rushed at her. Only the frantic waving of a Confederate flag convinced her crew not to open fire.

'Tuscaloosa' had not experienced much luck. In spite of the vigorous captaincy of Lt. Low, backed by his crew of eleven, their horizon had remained mostly empty, as had 'Alabama's during the same period. Only one success had come their way, the 'Santee', a slow moving rice transport, which had been bonded for $150,000.

The two Confederates sailed south together, 'Alabama' for Cape Town, 'Tuscaloosa' for Simon's Bay, and each arrived on the same day, the 5th of August. On the way, though, a chase had opened up for Semmes' ship, leaving 'Tuscaloosa' far behind. The barque 'Sea Bride' was spotted six miles from Cape Town itself, and if she had headed immediately for land, would have escaped into neutral waters. Even the Confederates had to respect international law when they could be watched. However, suspicions aboard the freighter were allayed, as usual, by the showing of a British flag, to the point that they took a diagonal course. Surprising this, because Captain Spalding of 'Sea Bride' had already once experienced capture by the raider 'Florida', and his officers were suspicious of the oncoming vessel. As it was, the capture of 'Sea Bride' was close enough to Cape Town to be observed with interest.

Among those onlookers, as it happened, was the United States Consul. He was not so passive in response as Captain Spalding, and complained vigorously about a breaking of neutrality laws. There had to be trouble, even with British authorities.

Perhaps Semmes should have burned his prize immediately, thus ending the matter. But he had found a valuable wool cargo on 'Sea Bride', like that on 'Tuscaloosa', and was reluctant to lose it. 'Sea Bride' was left anchored outside port, to await events and to be a constant reminder of the situation.

The British were in something of a quandary now. Accustomed to a natural sympathy for the Confederates, and with reports from other colonial ports of facilities granted to them, they were at the same time receiving information from home about the waning influence of the South through 1863. If opinion was swinging toward the United States, should they in Cape Town be helping Captain Semmes ? On top of all this came the news from Simonstown that no less than two other Confederate ships had arrived: The 'Georgia' and 'Tuscaloosa'. These were nominally warships, but 'Tuscaloosa' could be regarded as a prize of 'Alabama', and, if so, should not be allowed into their harbours. Pressed by the American consul, British Cape Town was being seen as anything but neutral. Nor was this situation helped by the enthusiastic welcome ashore for 'Alabama's crew.

While the authorities were thus wavering, Semmes was alerted to a real storm getting up at sea. Soon there were stories of ships being driven on to the rocks nearby, and he ordered the crew of 'Sea Bride' to take her away from the coast, and if things became too difficult, to rendezvous later with 'Alabama' further north at Angra Pequena.

By the 9th of August 'Sea Bride' had disappeared. 'Alabama' braved the storm to slip away to sea, heading north – a relief to the British, who had been seriously considering a move against her, but only a temporary relief, because 'Alabama' put into Simon's Bay the same day. Now the three Confederates were united.

Semmes, indeed, had little intention of staying away. Necessary repairs were incomplete, provisions still had to be obtained, and the 'Sea Bride's cargo sold. Semmes was rather contemptuous of the nervous attitude of the British officials. He knew nothing of the changing opinion in Britain, where Confederate influence was failing, nor did he appreciate the struggle between duty and inclination in those colonial officers, before whom Confederates were still regarded with admiration and respect. Thus he thought nothing of abusing privileges granted by the British, while at the same time accepting their hospitality. As for his Yankee opponents, his attitude was "Why do they insist that I go to sea, when every day costs them a ship ?".

At once 'Alabama' was visited by Admiral Walker, commander of the British Cape Fleet. He informed Semmes that a request for instructions had been sent to the government back in England. Consciences were clear. Until a reply was received, they could all stay in Cape waters, should they wish to do so.

Semmes, however, had other ideas, and continued to keep everyone guessing. Within three days, and in spite of poor weather and a defective water condenser, 'Alabama' and 'Tuscaloosa' left for their rendezvous at Angra Pequena. His intention, of course, was to meet a selected merchant there and to sell 'Sea Bride' and her cargo, together with the wool from 'Tuscaloosa', in a place far removed from the legal atmosphere of Cape

Town – Angra Pequena is a good 500 miles to the north.

In fact, the arrangement worked well. 'Sea Bride' had arrived as planned. The merchant arrived on a separate vessel, all deals were done and paid for, 'Alabama' received fresh water, and provisions were made up from the prizes.

Semmes now set off back to Cape Town, to get those repairs done, and to obtain a new condenser. Note how he was still taking the British for granted. 'Tuscaloosa', on the other hand, was sent off into the Atlantic on a second cruise of her own. Low decided on a sweep of the Brazilian coast.

Within a few days, 'Alabama' sailed straight into Simon's Bay. Was Semmes becoming over confident ? If so, the news awaiting him could not have been welcome. While the Confederates had been at Angra Pequena, the U.S.S. 'Vanderbilt' had been in to Cape Town and Simon's Bay, only to find the enemy gone. 'Georgia' had left very recently indeed. However, 'Vanderbilt' had been commissioned only to eliminate 'Alabama', and, released at last by Admiral Wilkes, she was doggedly determined to pursue her original purpose. Then, finding her target not far ahead, 'Vanderbilt' had left immediately for the Confederate rendezvous. Probably, the two had passed each other as 'Alabama' came south. Lucky, but little relief, because 'Vanderbilt' would certainly come straight back for her – with superior armament and speed this warship was to be avoided. Semmes must leave quickly, or be blockaded into surrender.

There was more. Admiral Walker advised that he would seize the 'Tuscaloosa' on her return, in accordance with the laws of neutrality. He was only awaiting positive support from the government, and expected that soon. It had been decided that the rebel prize was really a merchantman, her two guns not making up the armour of any sort of warship, and her captain was liable for prosecution for appearing in Simon's Bay. Semmes was helpless – he had to leave – and to leave the crew of 'Tuscaloosa' to their fate. When 'Vanderbilt' was reported close by, he sailed away from the Cape.

It was the 24th of September 1863. 'Alabama' headed east into the Indian Ocean, where no one expected her to go – certainly not the captain of 'Vanderbilt': and so she escaped capture yet again. Here we must leave the 'Alabama' story, with 'Tuscaloosa' soon to be captive, to consider the other Confederate raiders of 1863, and their varied success in the Atlantic Ocean.

Captain Maury of 'Georgia' had some success in the South Atlantic, taking three good prizes between June 13th and 27th. Two of those were burned, but the 'Constitution' carried coal, something always short in supply, and 'Georgia' laid alongside for a mid-ocean transfer. Unusually for such an operation, it was efficiently and completely accomplished, probably the most satisfactory offshore transfer the Confederates made.

At the beginning of August the rebel steamer approached the Cape of Good Hope, taking another prize on the way, and eventually halted for more refuelling in Simon's Bay. Truly, 'Georgia' used a lot of coal. Once there, of course, she became a stationary part of the 'situation' described above.

However, 'Georgia' had nothing to do with 'Alabama's campaign, so her departure on the 29th of August, which followed that of the other two Confederate cruisers, was incidental. A good thing, though, for within 16 hours the 'Vanderbilt' arrived. This Union warship would undoubtedly have been more than a match for 'Georgia', so it was lucky the former was interested only in 'Alabama', and would never deviate unless granted an easy opportunity.

No one really knew where 'Georgia' was going next, although rumours placed her in the West Indies or near Jamaica. In fact, she was heading due north, hoping still to make her name in the Atlantic, to shake off the slightly depressed feeling of the crew about their ship's performance. Two corn carriers were soon captured, and while Maury burned one, he released the 'Grisewold' on bond.

This apart, melancholy feelings of comparison with 'Alabama' persisted. Their elation from the Bahia meeting had long since evaporated, that coupled with bad news from the war itself, and the thought they might face piracy charges later on. On 'Alabama', where personal success overrode the larger issues, any bad news was passed over easily, but on 'Georgia' this was not so. The men felt unsafe. They expressed their feelings by discontent with the ship, her capability, the officers, and so on. In general they were at risk of becoming a bad crew.

However, it took a more serious incident, in which 'Georgia' came near to sinking, to convince one and all that their ship was ill-starred, and that they must leave her as soon as possible. This was the affair of the 'Bold Hunter'.

On October 9th, 1863, as 'Georgia' ploughed steadily northwards, she came across the United States full-rigged sailing ship the 'Bold Hunter' of Boston, out of Dundee with a full cargo of coal for Calcutta. After its capture, transfer of coal began, because 'Georgia' was as ever, short of fuel. Six complete trips with a small boat between the two had been accomplished, when the boat was nearly swamped. The business was at once halted – it was obviously too rough – and a decision taken to burn the prize. Accordingly the 'Bold Hunter' was set on fire, all prisoners being taken aboard 'Georgia'. At first all went well, clouds of smoke poured out, then flames hit the rigging, and swept up to the topmast, creating a considerable draught against the sails. . As none of those had been removed, they were quick to fill out before the sudden breeze. To the horror of all watching, the 'Bold Hunter' turned slowly until she was facing 'Georgia', then came rushing for the stationary raider. Hurriedly Maury ordered up sail – in vain, for the prize bore down too swiftly. The 3,000 ton coal ship rose almost straight above 'Georgia', then cracked solidly down on her quarter, cleaving plates and planks with a grinding shriek. Wooden splinters flew as lethal missiles, as men dived for cover. Confusion reigned. At one moment the flying jib stood right over 'Georgia's poop deck. Force pushed the cruiser off, while water poured into her stricken side, but the 'Bold Hunter' was not yet done. She came on again, striking this time a glancing blow, but sweeping port davits away and boats overboard. Yet again the 'Bold Hunter' charged, but this time the burning vessel had lost much way, and failed. She passed on, sails finally gone, masts falling, and came to a wallowing halt. In a vast cloud of steam the ship finally went down. It was only with difficulty that 'Georgia' got as far as Cherbourg by late October and limped into a hopefully friendly port.

In Cherbourg the men took their chance, many deserted the damaged and unlucky ship, while Maury himself fell seriously ill. John Evans now took over the captaincy, but although 'Georgia' remained a threat, obliging the United States to blockade her in Cherbourg, even Evans was unable to equip and crew her for another cruise. As 'Georgia' lay at Cherbourg, the best advice was to sell her.

What now of 'Florida', which after escaping from Mobile, had run into the Atlantic in spite of strenuous efforts to stop her. Indeed, Captain Maffit's luck had completely changed, because he continued to be successful. (Maffitt was promoted to Commander on the 29th of April 1863). From the 26th of February to the 10th of May 1863 he intercepted eight American merchantmen along the Brazilian coast, arriving on the last day in Pernambuco. This was the time 'Alabama' was creating similar havoc on a parallel course just to the north. Of the 'Florida's prizes six were burned, but two, the 'Lapwing' and 'Clarence', were equipped with guns and crew, to be used themselves as raiders. 'Lapwing' had yet another task, for she was carrying coal, and so was ordered to stay within a reasonable distance. In fact, the 'Lapwing' did actually take a prize, the 'Kate Dyer', which was bonded for $40,000, before meeting 'Florida' again by arrangement. For a while longer the two cruised together, but after all her coal had been transferred, it was decided to sink 'Lapwing' by burning.

'Clarence' served a different purpose. There was among Maffit's crew Midshipman Read, whose ambition, skill and determination exceeded the general run of officers. He proposed a daring plan, in which he would take the 'Clarence', a ship he regarded as excellent for his idea, into Chesapeake Bay to pick off army transports at anchor – there to support the Union Armies in Virginia: no telling how many could be destroyed, but certainly plenty. Maffit agreed with all this, so Read got his command. A howitzer and twenty men from 'Florida' were given him, and 'Clarence' sailed away to the north. More of her story later.

Staying only two days in Pernambuco, Maffit set off on his second phase of operations. He had heard of the intentions of Captain Semmes, but decided not to follow. He went north instead; after all, the North Atlantic was otherwise receiving little attention in 1863, and some trade could be expected off the United States coast. He may also have considered that, by doubling back, he would avoid his pursuers, undoubtedly not far behind him. In fact, he was lucky not to encounter 'Vanderbilt', finally released by the West Indies fleet and well on her way to the Cape.

Some really pleasant weather came next. The crew relaxed in the sunshine, bathed where possible, and only went to action stations at the infrequent sighting of a distant sail. Nothing wrong with that, of course. 'Florida's crew had the reputation of high efficiency during a chase and capture. Yet by report, Maffit allowed rather too much indiscipline at other times. Compared with 'Alabama', the sailors were poorly turned out and their ship was much more like a privateer than a naval vessel. Perhaps the worst result of such behaviour was the loss of morale when things weren't going well, whereas morale on 'Alabama' remained high throughout her two year cruise. Maffit was somewhat at the mercy of his men's emotions, where those captained by Semmes were always dependable.

For the moment, though, all was well for 'Florida', as a further five prizes fell her way through late May and June. Most of these were burned, although 'Varnum H. Hill' had to be bonded to carry the many prisoners to shore - the only solution to an ever-present problem.

Another matter arises here. Among the prizes burned was 'Red Gauntlet', an American ship carrying a neutral cargo. It was an unwritten rule accepted by the Confederates that such cargoes would be respected, and the ships bonded. Now, however, Maffit would seem to have broken the rule. His justification was that he had read captured newspapers reporting the American breaking of the bond on 'Ariel', taken by 'Alabama' in December 1862. 'Red Gauntlet' was burned as a reprisal: perhaps a sign of the coarsening effect of war.

By early July 'Florida' was approaching the north-eastern coast of the United States - when capturing and ransoming another cargo ship, the 'Sunrise' on the 8th of July (see next page for note on ransom bonds) she was only sixty miles from New York. Those were dangerous waters indeed. Once there, though, and anxious for quick success, Maffit began to look for local traffic, and when none appeared, sailed about rather aimlessly. He was not to know that 'Clarence' and Midshipman Read had already alerted the whole coastline. Indeed, 'Florida' had been sighted

- the reaction from shore was immediately to send out an armed ship to identify the stranger. Flying her United States colours the 'Ericcson' closed rapidly, came alongside, only to receive a deafening broadside from 'Florida' as the Confederate flag raced up her mast. 'Ericcson' staggered off, badly stricken and reeling from the shock. Fortunately thick fog fell just at that moment, making it possible for her to escape imminent destruction, and when it lifted, for her to be far enough away to avoid a chase. Maffit did try, but 'Florida' could disappointingly only raise ten knots, far too slow even for the 'Ericcson'. Partial success then for Maffit, but faster and more powerful warships would soon appear if 'Florida' remained. It was time to go.

While still close to New York, they did find and destroy two more small merchant ships, one so close to the shore that the crew escaped in a rowing boat, but in general there was nothing much to see. On the 16th of July 'Florida' put into Bermuda, ready for refuelling. On this occasion, the coal came from Halifax, Nova Scotia, by way of a tender, the 'Harriet Pinckney', organised by the Confederate agent there, and arriving in good time.

Maffit now resolved to take his ship across the Atlantic to a friendly French port, Brest, in Brittany, intending to end her cruise and his own involvement, and to hand over to the Confederate authorities based in France. Maffit knew his ship was fast wearing out. That failure to catch 'Ericcson' had certainly depressed him, but there were many signs of wear and tear – especially caused by the consistent shock of recoil from her guns. Maffit also felt unwell himself, and was disinclined to prolong the cruise. On to Brest then.

Two more prizes were taken in August, bringing the total bag for the spring and summer to 19 ships sunk, bonded or commissioned for the Confederates. From their point of view, a definite success, surely. During that cruise they had suffered only six casualties, not perhaps too high a price to pay, even though one had been the surgeon on board, Dr. Grafton.

Once in Brest, by September 3rd Maffit had left and most of the crew had been paid off. 'Florida' in its immobile state became part of the blockading responsibility of 'Kearsage'. However, the Confederates did not give up on her, as they would with 'Georgia'. They still had a ship of good potential at their disposal – once repairs had been completed 'Florida' could cruise again.

While 'Florida' was busy in the North Atlantic, her own appointment, the 'Clarence', had been engaged with Midshipman Read's plan.

Read was a graduate of Annapolis Naval Academy, having just completed his studies before the start of the war. Being an ardent supporter of the South, he joined their navy, and took part in the river

fighting around New Orleans. Later, he moved to Mobile, and was lucky
to be on hand when 'Florida' arrived there, desperately short of seamen.
Maffit immediately signed him on, and, as said above, was impressed – to
the point of giving him the command of 'Clarence'.

It took a matter of weeks for the new cruiser to reach the target area,
so their first prize, the 'Whistling Wind', was only taken on the 6th of
June, and that off the south-eastern coast of America. However, it was
followed by a spate of success. Two more ships, which turned out to be
coming south with supplies for the Union Army, were cut out on the 7th
and 9th respectively. As the army units stationed along the coast could
only be supplied by sea, a continuation of those victories would certainly
be significant – but Read was disconcerted by news passed on by them.
It was impossible for him to enter Chesapeake Bay. The entrance was
very closely guarded by strong warships, and one of 'Clarence's size and
armament had really no prospect of slipping through. Read therefore
resolved to patrol further north, in order to find, if possible, a ship with
clearance orders for the bay – perhaps deception would work.

In accordance with these plans, Read continued north, until, on the
12th of June, he sighted the sailing vessel 'Tacony', coming up fast. Read
hoisted a distress signal, and put out a rowing boat as though his ship was
in trouble. The 'Tacony' slowed to investigate, came over to 'Clarence',
and within minutes sailors from the latter were boarding and taking a
new prize in the name of the South. Read took a good look at his capture
and its papers. Here was his chance. He decided to change ships and to
burn 'Clarence'. However, before he could begin the shifting of guns
and ammunition, another ship was seen to be approaching. This was the
'M.A.Schindler', coming as though to help, and she finished by being
captured and burned. Then, suddenly, the 'Kate Stewart' followed, out
of curiosity, into the same trap. Eventually the Confederates had three
ships for their one manoeuvre, astonishing work for their sailors. 'Kate
Stewart' was bonded so that all the prisoners could be taken away.

Read now had to face the fact that he probably wouldn't be able to get
into Chesapeake Bay after all, even with 'Tacony' in place of 'Clarence'.
Their exploits would very quickly be too well known.

Even before the end of June, 'Tacony' had taken another fifteen prizes,
mainly fishing schooners – amazing that they had received no warning
of the raider. Were the northerners helpless against a smallish sailing ship
with one gun ? Amongst those prizes, indeed, was a still better prospect,
the schooner 'Archer', and once again Read made his switch. The 'Tacony'
was burned. By this time, the Union navy in receipt of so many reports,
must have been looking for a fleet of Confederates.

At this stage Read overreached himself. His northward cruise had
taken him to the coast of New England, and he next resolved to strike at
the important shipping harbour of Portland, Maine. Thus, by the 25th of

June the well disguised 'Archer' was idling off that port, as Read weighed up the possibilities. No one suspected his ship to be a Confederate, no one seemed to mind her presence in the shipping lanes. So unsuspicious were two men rowing past in a dinghy, that, when asked to come aboard, they happily agreed. Read told them they were prisoners of the Confederate States Navy – a joke, they thought, laughing heartily; and proceeded to tell Read everything about the Portland defences and the shipping present there, including a passenger liner, 'Chesapeake' and the revenue cutter 'Caleb Cushing', lying half deserted near the quay. At this information, Read was filled with enthusiasm. To cut out a government vessel…this was worth the risk, and just wait till they could tell the story back in Mobile.

The Confederates waited for darkness, and while the two talkative fishermen agreed to pilot 'Archer' in, Read explained his plan to the crew. The 'Chesapeake' was to be stolen from her moorings. All other craft would be burned, including the 'Caleb Cushing', while 'Archer' and 'Chesapeake' escaped back to sea.

In the darkened, crowded waterway they crept past the silent lines of shipping. At 1 a.m. the armed sailors threw themselves upon a startled group of men on the cutter, and 'Caleb Cushing' with its two guns was theirs. But everything else went wrong. His men took 'Chesapeake' as planned, but found the engines wouldn't work. She would have to be left, and the cutter taken instead. Unfortunately, the wind had by now nearly died, and the Confederate escape must be slow. As a result silence had to be maintained, so no destruction of other shipping could take place. 'Archer' began to creep out of harbour, against the current, escorting a similarly quiet 'Caleb Cushing'. Soon both ships were being pulled by rowing boat.

Progress was terribly slow, and by morning they were still in range of Portland's guns. Only an absence of gunners saved them then. It wasn't long, however, before some opposition was on its way. A steam powered side-wheeler, 'Forest City' and the familiar 'Chesapeake', her engines started by the regular crew, came straight for the slowly sailing Confederates. Both were well armed. A few rounds were fired back, but Read couldn't find the cutter's ammunition, and her imprisoned captain wouldn't tell him. It was all up, and Read surrendered his ships. His expedition had ended with him and all his crew going on to a northern prison camp. A disappointing end, then, but the 'Clarence'- 'Tacony'- 'Archer' had certainly caused quite a stir along the North American coast. The relief in New England was very great.

The year 1863 was undoubtedly most successful for the Confederate States Navy. It had begun with the West Indies Squadron's attempt to trap 'Florida' and 'Alabama' failing completely, as the two escaped easily into the Atlantic Ocean, while another Confederate cruiser, the 'Retribution', sailed successfully among those very islands. 'Alabama' had then swept the South Atlantic clear of United States shipping, with help from her offshoot, 'Tuscaloosa', and from a separate cruiser, the 'Georgia'. 'Florida' had dealt similar blows in the North Atlantic, and with 'Clarence', had terrorised the American coast as well. In late 1863 both main Confederate cruisers were undefeated whereas the United States carrying trade to Europe and South America had been nearly destroyed. As Gideon Welles himself said:

"The continued depredations of the rebel cruisers on the merchant marine of the country have not only destroyed a large amount of the active capital of the merchants, but seriously threaten the very existence of that part of our commerce".

Nor had the United States Navy distinguished itself. Welles again:

"The want of adequate armed vessels on prominent naval stations for protection of our ships has become so notorious that underwriters have no longer speculated on the chance of capture of these rebel cruisers by any of our national ships, but calculate only the chance of escape of our merchantmen, or the possible destruction of the piratical craft from reported unseaworthyness or mutiny".

It all sounds like complete victory for the South, but the Confederates had not achieved their most important objective, the removal of blockading warships from Southern ports, nor had they persuaded Britain or any other neutral country to come in on their side to break the blockade. Welles' policy had been maintained, and its favourable result would ultimately be fatal to the South. There was, of course, a large financial loss incurred by the Union, but that was born mainly by the merchants of New England, and did not affect the war.

Prize List of C.S.S. 'Georgia'

Name	Type	Date Taken (1863)	Fate
'Good Hope'	Barque	13th June	Burned
'Constitution'	Ship	25th June	Coal Ship
'City of Bath'		27th June	Burned
'J.W.Seaver'		June	Burned
'Dictator'	Ship	30th Sept	Burned
'Griswold'		30th Sept	Bonded
'Bold Hunter'	Ship	9th Oct	Burned
'Prince of Wales'		Oct	Burned
'John Watts'		Oct	Burned

RANSOM BONDS

The capture of 'Sunrise' by C.S.S. 'Florida' serves to illustrate the form of ransom bond taken from prizes when they are released under those conditions. The company, to which the prize belongs, forfeits an amount stipulated in the bond to the Confederate Government, and is required to make good the debt at the end of the war.

The Bond

"This bond, made and entered into this seventh day of July, 1863, by and between Richard Luce, master and commander of the American ship 'Sunrise' of the first part, and John N. Maffitt, Lt. Commanding in the Navy of the Confederate States of America of the second part, witnesseth:

"That the said party of the first part is held and firmly bound (for himself, the ship and the owners) unto Jefferson Davis, President of the Confederate States of America, or his successors in office, in the full and penal sum of $60,000, to be well and truly paid, in gold or its equivalent, within six calendar months after a ratification of a treaty of peace between the Confederate States and the United States.

"The condition of this bond is such that the aforesaid of the first part has this day been captured on the high sea, while in command of the ship aforesaid, by the Confederate States sloop-of-war 'Florida', whereof the party of the second part is commander, and has been allowed to proceed on his voyage without injury or detriment to the ship or cargo, and has been guaranteed against molestation during the present voyage from any and all armed vessels in the service of the Confederate States of America.

"Done in duplicate aboard the Confederate States sloop-of-war 'Florida', the day and date above written.

"Witness:	Thomas Barry	Richard Luce (seal)
	1st Officer	Master commanding
"Witness:	G.D.Bryan	J.N. Maffitt
	Midshipman C.S.N.	Lt. Commanding, C.S.N.

Movements & Dispositions of U.S. Warships (ex-blockade)
September 1862 - August 1863

CHAPTER EIGHT

'Alabama' in the Indian Ocean

The 'Tuscaloosa' returned to Cape Town on the 26th of December 1863, after as disappointing a cruise as fell to a Confederate Naval vessel all through the war. For ninety days she had searched again those routes covered previously by the 'Alabama', from the Cape right up to the coastal waters of Brazil, and had seen only one American ship out of one hundred questioned. Even that one carried a British cargo, and was therefore inviolate: such was the effect of 'Alabama's passage. However, what was even more disappointing to Lt. Low, the captain of 'Tuscaloosa', was the seizure of his ship as it entered harbour. He hadn't known of the last decisions given to Semmes. There was nothing for Low and his officers to do but pack their bags for Europe, there to join the pool of Confederate naval officers waiting for employment.

'Alabama' had indeed left earlier, on the 24th of September specifically, pressured by the near presence of 'Vanderbilt' and with no opportunity to warn Low: and as mentioned in Chapter 7, headed east through the Indian Ocean.

Why go east ? There were reasons for such a novel strategy, of course. Captain Baldwin of 'Vanderbilt' might not expect it, and might go in the wrong direction as a result. Again, Semmes knew the Atlantic had been well visited, so perhaps better rewards might be gained elsewhere – and no Confederate raider had been to the Far East. Equally, there weren't going to be many US warships there.

Perhaps, also, Semmes was influenced by events at home. He must have known by September 1863 that the war was going badly, and that his government's naval policy had not so far opened Southern ports. Semmes was tactically far from the Confederacy, and there was no one to guide his decisions. Indeed, one reason for choosing him as captain in the first place was an ability to think and act independently. He must therefore have reasoned that if clearing the Atlantic of American ships had had no effect, possibly some damage to American trade in the east might just make a difference; and his crew followed him unquestioningly, because to them Semmes was the Confederacy.

However, leaving Simon's Town when he did, took 'Alabama' into extremely rough weather, gales that had already driven a variety of ships ashore at the Cape. Nobody had time to think about motives as they ploughed through towering seas and high winds. For two weeks this went on, until all were numb with the battering. Yet they made 2400 miles to the east in that time, well to the south of their intended track, and passing the remote islands of St.Peter and St.Paul, fully 1000 miles from any land. Finally conditions calmed to a gentle breeze, allowing Semmes to change course north, on the way to the Sunda Straits. 'Vanderbilt' had tried to pursue, but imagining Semmes would head for British territory, sailed to Mauritius. Finding nothing there, and with a whole ocean to choose from, Captain Baldwin headed back to the Atlantic.

By this time the U.S.S. 'Wyoming', sole United States naval vessel in the far east, and guardian of their rice, jute and China tea trade interests, had been alerted. Thus, when 'Alabama' approached her first landfall, at Java, 'Wyoming' was positioned in the Sunda Straits between Java and Sumatra. Strangely, though, the two never did meet, possibly because the American persisted in chasing reports of 'Alabama's sighting, and was therefore always behind. If she had worked by anticipation, things might have worked out differently. Nor did Semmes shrink from their meeting. After the 'Hatteras' sinking, he felt 'Alabama' to be equal to most Union warships, and 'Wyoming' was certainly not the largest they had.

As it was, the sudden appearance of the fabled 'Alabama' in eastern waters caused a wholesale panic among ship owners, captains and crews, what with the rumours that all prisoners were automatically executed by drowning. No great confidence in 'Wyoming' was felt, either. Within a week nearly every United States ship was laid up in port, in Singapore or Bangkok, refusing to come out at all. Trade slid to a graceless standstill, while cargoes were transferred to neutrals.

From the 10th of November until almost the end of the year, 'Alabama' cruised through the East Indies, taking only six prizes – and even with those six there was an element of luck. 'Amanda' was captured in the Sunda Strait, before any warning had got about. 'Contest' was a fast sailing ship, one of the well known China clippers, whose captain considered was definitely able to outrun 'Alabama'. Sadly for him, the wind died away completely, and 'Contest' was overtaken by steam. The 'Martaban' was skilfully disguised as a neutral, and it took all the skill and experience of Semmes to show her documents were not in order. She was, in fact, the American merchantman 'Texas Star', a name that came to light when her newly painted name had been scraped off. All six prizes were burned, after yielding valuable quantities of fresh provisions.

Otherwise 'Alabama' had a picnic voyage, met at every port by swarms of traders with tempting goods. The sailors ate as well as they ever had, and in the warm weather sickness fell to a negligible level. No fighting at all was necessary.

After looping back in the South China Sea, Semmes called at the island of Pulo Condore (the Condore Islands are just off the coast of Vietnam, and in 1863 were French colonial property). Here he found a friendly reception from the French settlers and was able to rest for some patching of the hull, together with badly needed cleaning in 'Alabama's boilers.

To the French the visitors were a welcome diversion from their own problems – including a recent native uprising quelled by government troops. Those natives were essentially slaves, so could hardly have been attracted by 'Alabama' and her Southern crew. On the other hand, that position would serve to give the settlers common cause with Semmes. They certainly looked after the Confederates, too, bringing plentiful supplies of provisions, including some very acceptable fresh meat. The sailors had a pleasant time on the warm, lush island.

On one occasion they were all invited to a hunting expedition, when someone was inconsiderate enough to shoot a baboon. Those creatures do have some near-human characteristics, and had been coming to the shore to stare at 'Alabama' ever since her arrival. When the shooting occurred the animals did not run away, but gathered round the corpse to show their misery. One of the larger baboons then dug a grave, and their comrade was buried amid much lamentation. After that they returned to the jungle, apparently satisfied that duty had been done.

On the 15th of December 'Alabama' left for Singapore, meeting in the next few days a variety of foreign vessels, all to be checked out, but none from the United States. Semmes was fairly dissatisfied by this, because he knew the American ships were being held back in port. The Confederates were having little success. Not that the crew were too worried. As they were passing the numerous small islands in that part of the world, small boats of all descriptions would come out to offer fruits, nuts, and local produce of all kinds. It was a good time for the sailors.

Singapore was reached on the 21st of December, 'Alabama' following another steamer into the packed, jumbled harbour. Again they were made welcome, this time by the British, whose pilot boat led them in. Singapore was already in 1863 a rapidly expanding entrepot, where ships of every nation – except, of course, the United States, were busy loading or unloading. Semmes now heard that 'Wyoming' had been in Singapore recently, so he decided not to stay long. Indeed, the Far Eastern trip had been to his thinking so unsuccessful, he resolved to return directly via the Malacca Straits and across the Indian Ocean to Cape Town: and so he did.

In fact, the Straits proved rather more rewarding, because three prizes were taken in their passage, and in getting rid of the prisoners, Semmes even found time to call at the pretty Malayan village of Malacca. By New Year's Day 1864 'Alabama' was well on her way in the Indian Ocean in hot, sunny weather. Her effect and reputation lasted much longer. It was months before American shipping stirred again, so great was the fear that she would return.

Within a fortnight 'Alabama' was off the Malabar Coast, almost becalmed, and seeking another period of rest. She had more prisoners, too, from the 'Emma Jane' – her 62nd prize, picked up along the way. On the 16th of January the Ghaut Mountains came in sight, their first view of ancient India. On the same day they dropped anchor in Angenga Roads, to the great surprise and excitement of the population, unused to seeing ships there. Angenga was a port with history, originally there to serve inland Travancore, when that state had been rich and important, but in 1864 of little significance. (There was, in any case, no harbour at Angenga, so that all cargo had to be carried through the surf by small but stout rowing craft). All cargo now went through Cochin, 50 miles away. However, Semmes wanted to unload his prisoners, and certainly didn't want to waste time going on up the coast. He sent Lt. Wilson ashore with 'Emma Jane's crew to arrange for their onward transport to Cochin.

After a short but restful stay, Semmes followed a course from India to bring him along the eastern seaboard of Africa, then southward towards the Cape. Three weeks sailing, mostly against a northerly breeze and relying often on steam, brought him to the Comoro Islands, between Madagascar and Mozambique: but disappointingly had given him no prizes.

At Comoro the crew found themselves once again greeted with enthusiasm. The islands were nominally controlled by the French, though loosely so, but the behaviour of local people had little appeal for Confederate officers. When invited to a church service, they were embarrassed to be listening to a sermon on the evils of slavery. Semmes became anxious to be away, and as soon as they had purchased enough fresh food to load up their ship, the Confederates weighed anchor for the Cape.

Another uneventful month saw them approaching Cape Town, making slow progress against the very winds they had experienced six months before. Indeed, they were in some danger from other ships sailing east, who came full tilt toward them on the gale, without much chance of manoeuvring. On the 11th of March 'Alabama' was in sight of the Cape, yet it was the 20th before they could attempt to get into safe shelter. Then, with spray crashing over their ship, and with decks flooded, the bruised and battered rebel cruiser limped into Table Bay. After those pleasant encounters in the east, it was back to reality for the Confederates.

Had it all been a waste of time ? Semmes might have thought so, having taken only eight prizes in the period. However, the effect on United States trade had been considerable, as mentioned already, and even as 'Alabama' lay in Cape Town, 'Wyoming' was still hunting for her in the East Indies, while the Chinese government was being warned not to receive her into Chinese ports. No, large financial losses had been and still were being imposed upon the Americans, as long as their ships stayed in port. From the point of view of Confederate policy, the excursion had been well worth their effort.

Whatever his feelings about that, though, Semmes was angry to hear the news of 'Tuscaloosa'. As described above, that ship had been arrested in Simon's Town, and the crew had gone back to Europe. Soon after they left, a further message came in from England, reversing the decision, presumably on the grounds that, after all, 'Tuscaloosa' should be considered a warship. The Confederate must be released immediately. The fair-minded Admiral Walker tried to carry out his instructions, but could find no-one to take responsibility or control. So matters stood when Semmes and the Confederates reappeared from the sea. For a brief moment Walker was delighted. Then Semmes amazed him by refusing to take 'Tuscaloosa', declaring that the British had so severely tried his patience by seizing the ship, he would not now relieve them of the burden of disposal. In any case he had no crew to spare.

Now this might inconvenience the British, but the Confederacy could ill afford such a gesture. 'Tuscaloosa' was quite suitable for its task, was in a good state of repair, and could have been satisfactorily manned by a few men for the journey to Europe, escorted by 'Alabama'. Once in the north, the Confederate agents would be most grateful for another cruiser, at a time when they were finding it difficult to build or fit out any ships for their purpose; and there were plenty of Confederate naval officers available. Perhaps the strain of his long cruise was beginning to cloud Semmes' judgement. Perhaps, too, the condition of his own ship was a consideration. 'Alabama' was fairly worn out by the endless battering of the sea, by the violent accelerations needed to catch those fleeing merchant ships, and by the changes in climate. Her boilers were in poor shape, her frame was leaking, her bottom copper plating peeling off in rolls. Her maximum speed was much reduced, while only emergency repairs had been made. They must return to Europe, and probably to France, their best friend now. Fresh Confederate funds would see to the rebuilding of 'Alabama'.

On the 25th of March, 1864, therefore, they left Cape Town, and by the 10th of June were in the vicinity of Cherbourg.

CHAPTER NINE

French Intervention

In Chapter 4 the British part in the American Civil War was described. That was built around common interests, a need for cotton in British mills, and resentment at American tariffs against European goods. France was in much the same situation in 1861, having herself a large manufacturing industry, including many cotton mills, and with a population sympathetic after its own fight for freedom fifty years before. She also could have advantages from breaking a blockade of Southern ports, and thus would tend to support Confederate attempts to create a viable navy. Though a colonial power with plenty of friendly ports of call for Southern ships, France did not have as much control on the sea as Britain had, but made it plain that her policy toward the Confederacy would be the same. Breaking the blockade would depend on the British fleet, but France would offer diplomatic support and facilities at her home ports. If Britain finally recognised the Confederacy as a nation, so also would France.

The Confederacy tried to build on this support as they had in Britain. Thus, when James Bulloch was sent to Liverpool, his equivalent sent to Paris was Samuel Barron: and don't forget that in the Mason and Slidell affair, Slidell was intended to be the Confederate representative in France. Many hopes were built on the latter's influence.

The most important strand in France's policy, however, was the ambition of their leader, the Emperor Napoleon the Third, aiming at the conquest and occupation of Mexico. That republic had been unstable territory since independence from Spain, and had incurred huge debts in Europe – especially in France. Because the Mexican government was weak, attempts to solve those problems had from time to time involved foreign troops, but no-one had so far been successful in establishing firm control. Now in 1862 the only foreign troops present were French. Napoleon saw his opportunity. Yet he knew the United States would object to a total conquest up to their border and would probably intervene physically. If a friendly Confederacy, recognised by France and able to trade with her, stood between, his Mexico could become much more practical. Napoleon's strategy, therefore, was to press for a declaration of Southern independence. The only restraint upon him was the influence of his ministers, who knew that no action without Britain would be effective. Hence they must wait upon the latter, offering the South until then only the level of assistance given in Britain. Through the year 1862 that situation was maintained.

By early 1863 an impatient Napoleon could wait no longer. French forces in Mexico were reinforced, and began to overrun the country. Early and complete victory seemed likely. On the other hand, the Confederacy for its part was certainly not doing as well. By mid 1863 the whole length of the Mississippi had been lost to Union forces, and their country cut in two. Everything to the west of the river, essentially Texas, had been isolated, and was fighting on alone. But Napoleon was not deterred. He imagined an additional though separate agreement with the state of Texas, in which his part would be to help the latter to survive: and the best help he was in a position to give straight away was to support more strongly the Confederates in Europe.

Napoleon was conscious of the growing disquiet in England about Confederate cruisers, and that building or supplying them would get steadily more difficult there. He therefore (as a neutral !) quietly invited Barron to build some in France. Through the recommendations and influence of Slidell, in 1863 contracts were placed with Armans of Bordeaux and Nantes for clipper corvettes, each to have ten cannon, and iron-clad steamers, to have one Armstrong rifle and two 70 lb turret guns: six ships in all - power, indeed. If such vessels broke loose, they could well have a decisive effect. In a step even less neutral than had ever been considered in Britain, the French government agreed to arm, equip and supply these ships. Such was Napoleon's enthusiasm at that time. In the second half of 1863 France was definitely seen as most favoured European refuge for the Confederates.

That influenced the cruisers at sea, because all of them required some dockyard attention after an exhausting campaign. No doubt the Confederacy had been hoping to use home ports by now, but the plan to free them from blockade had not worked. Britain had become decidedly neutral, and while France was nominally so, there was a definite bias at work; if a belligerent's ships sought and needed repair, they could stay in France.

On September 3rd the 'Florida' arrived in Brest, followed in October by 'Georgia' coming into Cherbourg, and in November by 'Rappahannock' into Calais, after her escape from Britain. All these, together with the ships being built at Bordeaux and Nantes, were opposed by one United

States warship stationed off the French coast, the 'Kearsage': and, surprisingly, no others were sent. Union policy was still giving priority to their Southern blockade.

U.S.S.'Kearsage' has appeared before in this story, during the blockade of 'Sumter' in Gibraltar. Following that, she had cruised about the Azores in 1862, as part of the search for 'Alabama'. Then followed four months in Cadiz for repairs – in a neutral country with more affinity than France for the United States: at which point she was joined by her new captain John Winslow. The 'Kearsage' was a second class ship by American standards, not having the speed or manoeuvrability of later models, but her armament could match any of the Confederate raiders. Now her task was to patrol off the coasts of Europe, hoping to deter Southern activity: a rather onerous employment, in the circumstances. However, Winslow's orders were loose, and with considerable freedom of action. When 'Florida', 'Georgia' and 'Rappahannock' arrived, 'Kearsage' was immediately placed in a position to cover all three ports from the head of the English Channel.

In return Sam Barron devised a December plan for the Confederates. The 'Florida', nearly ready for sea, would hold 'Kearsage' off Brest, while 'Georgia' and 'Rappahannock' slipped out to come up behind her. Caught between these three, the 'Kearsage' would be battered to pieces. Perhaps that would persuade the European powers to declare for the South.

Unfortunately, the plan had serious flaws. 'Georgia' was scarcely fit for sea. 'Rappahannock' had no guns, and was only just capable of maintaining herself away from harbour. Worse still, her abrupt departure from Britain had been made without clearance, and, under pressure from the English, she was actually being detained by a French gunboat in Calais.

Now, that matter might have been overcome if Napoleon's government had remained true to their previous statements. But by December 1863 the capricious mind of Napoleon was on the move. His campaign in Mexico had gone so well, he no longer felt the need for allies. The move to attract Texas into an agreement had come to nothing, and he could see that the Confederacy was in any case losing the war. He began to withdraw support in France itself – his position enabling him to take such decisions without consulting anyone else.

The Confederates were soon undermined. Orders went out that 'Florida' and 'Georgia' were to leave French harbours as soon as repairs were complete. 'Rappahannock' was to be restrained from leaving at all. But that wasn't all. In September 1863 the United States minister in Paris, William Dayton, had discovered the destination of the six ships building in Bordeaux and Nantes. At first the Emperor would not listen, but with the change of heart in December, the Americans were able to press forward their arguments. In March 1864 Napoleon finally ordered the interruption of those very contracts he had so urgently approved. The Arman ships were sold off to other nations, leaving the Confederacy 5 million francs poorer, and with six good ships lost to their cause.

Barron was now thoroughly alarmed by the reports from a bewildered John Slidell. He was obliged immediately to give up his first plan – the crushing of 'Kearsage', and to concentrate on getting 'Florida' out before there was any interference. However much the officials in charge at the ports were still sympathetic, the word of Napoleon was final.

In the absence of Captain Maffitt, the command of 'Florida' in Brest had devolved upon Captain Barney from the officers' pool. It was he who had seen to the repairs on shaft, copper lining and steam blower, equipment whose condition had inconvenienced the cruiser earlier. Another problem he dealt with was provision of a crew, for the original sailors had all been paid off. More had to be smuggled on to the ship in small groups, something flagrantly against the laws of neutrality. Tension surrounded the docks in Brest as rumours flew, and bribes were distributed. As the new attitudes in France created even more pressure on Barney, he struggled to win sufficient supplies of coal. In the end his own health collapsed. Yet another officer, Lt. Charles Morris, came from the pool on the 11th of January 1864 to take 'Florida' to sea.

By mid January 1864 'Florida's repairs and subsequent trials were complete. Now it was a matter of avoiding 'Kearsage', still posted out beyond the harbour. The Confederates knew they only had to wait, because every ship requires reprovisioning and refuelling at some time. That time came in February, when 'Kearsage' abandoned her watch for a quick trip to Cadiz, hoping to return before anything happened. It was too much to ask, of course, and there was no other cover. 'Florida' sailed out unchallenged on the 10th of February. Six days later 'Georgia' was hurried out too, and when 'Kearsage' came back from Cadiz, two of her enemies had gone.

In fact, 'Georgia' had not gone far. A new plan, involving the escape of 'Rappahannock', and the transfer of 'Georgia's guns to her, had been put into action by Sam Barron. Unfortunately, it had proved impossible to persuade the authorities in Calais, and 'Rappahannock' couldn't move. When 'Kearsage' returned she had only one ship to bother with, and seal it up she did. That was the end for 'Rappahannock', and in March the confederates gave up trying a rescue. The potential raider was converted into a depot ship, and played no real part in the war.

The 'Georgia' as mentioned above, was really unfit for further service. Although her captain, Lt. Maury, back after his serious illness, was able to take her out of Cherbourg, his intention had been to unload his guns before making final decisions. His advice was a quick sale.

Even the gun transfer hadn't happened, when 'Rappahannock' failed to rendezvous. On the 24th of March, despairing of the plan, Maury put in at Bordeaux, with the idea of awaiting Barron's orders. However, no word came, while, on the 28th of April he was ordered out by the French – no longer tolerant of his ship. That left Maury to think about a last cruise to the Mediterranean, untouched by the Confederates so far, with a possible diversion to the Moroccan coast. Not a good idea: 'Georgia' simply wasn't up to it.

Eventually and with regret the old raider was taken to Liverpool, where in May she was sold. All warlike equipment was taken off and the crew dismissed. 'Georgia' left Liverpool as the legitimate property of a British merchant. Amazingly, and for the first time, she was intercepted off Lisbon by the U.S.S.'Niagara'. The American took no chances, removing 'Georgia' to the United States, and ending her career once and for all. No compensation was paid to the merchant, who thus became the main loser.

That was really the end of the French intervention. Hopes had been high, but hopes had been dashed. It all showed how dependent were the Confederates on foreign help. Their navy had no available ports of its own, at least until the blockade was broken, and that never happened. Without the assistance of a European power, their naval war could not be won.

Then the sudden arrival of 'Alabama' in the port of Cherbourg made Barron, Slidell and the officers' pool forget for a moment the problems of the Confederate Navy. With their champion at hand, high drama was surely imminent.

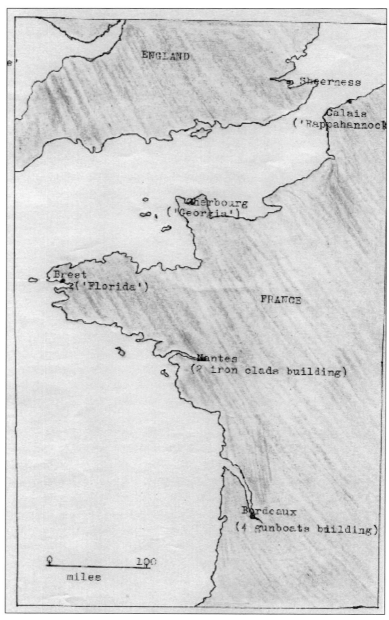

Confederate use of French ports - December 1863

CHAPTER TEN

The Battle between 'Kearsage' & 'Alabama'

It must have been a nasty shock for Raphael Semmes and his crew to discover how things had changed in France. All those good reports about an enthusiastic welcome – all were completely out of date. No question, he had been looking forward to a rest and relaxing holiday, when 'Alabama' could be properly repaired. How they had earned it; no one had done more for the good of the Confederacy – and, even in their slightly worn out condition, they had worked hard for their cause. Two prizes had been taken on the way north, one, the 'Rockingham', used for target practice for 'Alabama's gunners, the other burned (making 64 in all for the two year cruise). However, that didn't describe the level of work required. In truth, very few American merchant ships were available to capture now, a lasting consequence of those encounters with Confederate cruisers. 'Alabama' had in fact chased no fewer than 19 ships for their two successes – the remainder were under neutral flag. Now, even staying in Cherbourg would be difficult. Semmes was entitled by the laws of neutrality to ask for time to do necessary repair work; and he found he could buy coal from the dockside facility. But the Emperor Napoleon made everything else as difficult as possible – he delayed a request for 'Alabama' to go into dry dock, for instance - in spite of his subordinates' willingness to cooperate.

The blockade by 'Kearsage' was another disconcerting problem. That warship had come straight to Cherbourg on hearing the news, Captain Winslow being happy to abandon the futile watch on 'Rappahannock': and, after all, 'Alabama' was the cruiser every American sailor wanted to sink.

Faced with frustration in France, and obviously unable to escape without confrontation, Semmes turned instead to the chance of a fight. Taking a small boat, he and his officers examined 'Kearsage' closely. Their conclusion: the American ship was no stronger than their own, and certainly could be beaten. 'Kearsage' was not one of their best warships, not a 'Vanderbilt', which by repute would be too powerful.

Semmes did feel confident. They had destroyed the 'Hatteras', of course, and the recent firing practice against 'Rockingham' told him the skill of those days was present still. Then again there was the prestige to be gained. All those people who criticised 'Alabama' as a pirate ship, capable only of attacking defenceless merchant ships, ought to be shown how a warship of the Confederate States Navy could fight. After the series of land defeats in 1863, a victory at sea would do something to raise morale all round, and Semmes had a good case for taking on the 'Kearsage'.

However…however, should he have done that? The battle could go either way, because the ships were evenly matched, and while 'Kearsage' was just one of a large fleet, 'Alabama' stood alone, indispensable to her country, and given the situation in Europe, not easy to replace. Perhaps it was another sign of Semmes' tiredness that he let himself go with his emotions here.

For Captain Winslow there were no hesitations. Few United States Naval commanders in the Civil War had opportunity for a direct engagement. There were few enough ships in the Confederate Navy, and those did their best to keep out of the way. Nor was he worried about relative gun capability. 'Kearsage' was well able to hold her own, especially if the fight was at short range. Moreover she had a secret weapon, because over the sides of 'Kearsage' special chain-mail armour was draped. That sounds almost mediaeval, but it did give effective protection against the penetration of shot and shell – not noticed by Semmes during his inspection. Winslow was all for battle.

On both sides, therefore, the decision was made. Semmes sent word through the US Consul Bonfils that the Confederate States Navy was challenging the United States Navy to a duel outside the harbour of Cherbourg; the battle to be on Sunday the 19th of June 1864 (see note 1). Thus there was to be no rush to gain surprise, nor could battle be refused by the Confederates. Semmes was committed, and was fully backed up by his officers and crew.

The morning of the 19th dawned bright and clear, but there was none of the usual quiet. Word of the duel had spread widely, and people were pouring into Cherbourg. Excitement had been growing from day to day – all significance of the outcome was lost in the competition for seats or standing room along the shore and in the harbour.

Last preparations had proceeded swiftly on 'Alabama'. Many volunteers had been received on board to make up crew numbers. Urgent repairs were put aside for afterwards, while only patching to keep the ship afloat was carried through. Sufficient coal to fill all their bunkers was hastily loaded – good idea; the weight of coal would keep the ship relatively low in the water, and a smaller target; might also absorb some of the damaging shellfire. Semmes made an impassioned speech. Then 'Alabama' left the quay, surrounded by a swarm of little boats, from schooners to skiffs, only losing them as she turned across the Cherbourg breakwater by the west pass. At once the great crowd of onlookers fell silent.

'Kearsage' was about five miles out, having withdrawn to ensure 'Alabama' had to come a long way from her protective anchorage. 'Alabama' surged on, straight for her adversary, her Confederate 'stars and bars' streaming from the masthead, her boilers supporting the sails to the limit. After her came the 'Couronne', a French ironclad, though this dropped steadily behind to stay out of harm's way. Then it was "Gun ports open. Ready to fire".

At ten minutes past eleven the 'Alabama' commenced circling in a clockwise direction, for her intention was to steer well wide of 'Kearsage', employing her long range guns, and preventing the other getting too close. Winslow had some powerful short range guns. Simultaneously 'Alabama' opened the battle with a 100 pound gun from the bow. The ships wore about their circles, about a mile apart, and 'Kearsage's starboard battery, in spite of the difficulty in aiming, started its reply. At once the Confederate ensign was shot from its masthead.

Seven times did the adversaries circle about each other, while the fight swayed equally between them. One shell from 'Alabama' crashed splinteringly into the sternpost of 'Kearsage', but failed to explode – had it done so, the battle would have been over. Another shell tore away part of her upper works.

The damage on 'Alabama' was, however, much worse. One shell hammered against the cabin work; another blew up a complete gun crew, knocking the gun irretrievably askew. Only now did Semmes finally see the chain mail, against which his shells were exploding harmlessly. He called for a change to shot, but hard as the gunners worked, their aim was way off. In the end, though, it was the powder which let them down. While a cloud of white, puffy smoke rose above 'Kearsage', smoke made by 'Alabama' hung heavy, black and dull along the cruiser's bulwarks. The sound of their exploding cannon was never a crisp crack, but a muted roar, a certain sign that the powder was defective. Two years' storage had taken their toll. It meant that the power of 'Alabama' was severely restricted, and this could only be emphasised as devastating volleys from the 'Kearsage' broke into her waterline timbers. Water poured in.

Soon all that Semmes could see through the smoke were dark, blackened faces, and all he could hear were the cries of wounded. On the other hand he could feel the new sluggish motion of his ship, and that it was beginning to list. Nor was all well with the engines.

Semmes realised that he had many casualties. The guns were no longer working effectively, and he needed to concentrate what men he had left. He ordered some forward from the rear to man the gaps. But their response was slow, and Semmes knew too that morale had gone – it was a struggle only for survival. The ship staggered under more shellfire, and a mast came crashing to the deck. All this while their opponent remained unaffected. The fight was lost. He determined to run for shore. At exactly twelve noon, 'Alabama' withdrew. As a witness reported, "At twelve a slight intermission was observed in the 'Alabama's fire, the 'Alabama' making head sail, and shaping her course for the land, distance about nine miles". (This report was from the 'Deerhound', a British pleasure yacht – where had she come from ?).

Even as Semmes applied this measure, Engineer Freeman came rushing from below to report the fires out, swamped by fast inrushing sea. Semmes sent Lt. Kell, his most trusted officer, to estimate the damage. Surely the great 'Alabama' was not about to sink !

The manoeuvre to port had placed 'Alabama' in an even worse position. With resistance dying and coordination lost, she was now exposed to a full raking fire from 'Kearsage'. 'Alabama' came to a sinking halt, just as Kell returned to report a hopeless situation. Semmes did not hesitate. He struck his colours, hauling up the white flag of surrender, calling on the crew to abandon ship. That was none too soon, for 'Alabama' was leaning heavily, large pieces of wood and iron were sliding across the deck, and everyone standing was groping about to stay upright. Two lifeboats were launched through all the chaos, and while one was rowed over to 'Kearsage' for help, the second was reserved for wounded – surgeon Galt in charge. 'Alabama' now sank quickly, amid the explosions of ammunition and shouts from men leaping into the sea. Semmes was the last to go, flinging his sword away as a gesture of defiance. Its polished metal shone once more in the sunlight as it splashed down, then vanished for ever. 'Alabama' too was gone, leaving on the surface a fearful scattering of bodies, masts, splinters and all the paraphernalia of a ship.

All attention now turned to the survivors struggling to stay alive. 'Kearsage' was understandably slow in getting her boats away. After the surrender signal had been made by 'Alabama', it seems that a few final shots were fired from the raider. Captain Winslow had to be certain no fresh trickery was afoot, so he drew off a little and hesitated, giving a chance to the yacht mentioned above, the 'Deerhound', to get in close. Indeed, if she had not, many might have drowned. As it was, a good number of the Confederate sailors escaped to her, while two handily placed French pilot boats also did noble work. Winslow, on the other hand, was to be criticised later for not gathering in all his prisoners - definitely an unjust claim in the circumstances.

The boat full of prisoners, with surgeon Galt, did reach 'Kearsage', while in the confusion and undignified scramble, Lt. Wilson, who surrendered his sword, and engineer Freeman were the only other officers taken aboard by her. For the most part, in fact, 'Deerhound' steered unerringly through the mess to pick up the remaining officers – no fewer than 14 of them, including Semmes and Kell, and rescued 27 seamen as well. All these were dropped off eventually in a British port, leading inevitably to the accusation that 'Deerhound' had been hired as a standby for 'Alabama', and to Winslow's rage at his incomplete victory. He only captured 60 men out of 150 involved, and with them the three officers mentioned. All other survivors were carried away into Cherbourg by the

French – there to disappear. Because of the confusion, it is uncertain how many died in the battle, but probably 16 on the Confederate side. Only three men on the 'Kearsage' were wounded, of which one died.

What was the 'Deerhound's role ? She seems to have been what was claimed, a yacht owned by John Lancaster of Wigan, England, which just happened to be in Cherbourg at the time. But her subsequent behaviour has been compromised, because Winslow said he asked Lancaster to help pick up survivors. Perhaps there was a misunderstanding, but Winslow also said he expected those rescued to be brought to 'Kearsage', and when they were not, he was completely frustrated. Winslow later accused the British of rescuing Semmes and his officers from a possible charge of piracy.

On 'Kearsage', however, Winslow now found that he certainly could not hold all the prisoners he did have, for reasons of supply. He was himself isolated off the French coast. He therefore paroled nearly all of them, including the wounded, not to fight against the United States again, and kept back three, Engineer Freeman, Assistant Engineer Pundt and Boatswain McCaskey – no doubt because they failed to make that promise. Even so, Winslow lost one of those, when, on a visit to Dover, he allowed Pundt to go ashore under a temporary parole to see a doctor. Pundt failed to return. Winslow had only two for Northern prison camps when he got back to America

'Deerhound', in the meantime, arrived in Southampton, where Lancaster handed over his precious cargo to an enthusiastic hero's welcome. But, amid the celebrations at his arrival on neutral territory, Semmes certainly picked up the suggestions made by Winslow on his behaviour. Particularly, he was worried at any charges of piracy, from which 'Deerhound' had saved him – Semmes conducted a correspondence through the Times in his defence.

Being unable to arrest Semmes, Winslow argued back. Many statements were made by both sides as to the conduct of the battle, making an unseemly end to the affair. However, nothing could change the fact that 'Kearsage' had won a notable victory – Winslow gained enormous credit at home for that. The 'Alabama' legend had been broken, the invincibility of the Southern cruisers brought down to earth, and the pride and reputation of the United States Navy restored.

'Kearsage' was soon relieved on her lonely station by the sloop 'Iroquois'. She had relatively few scars, and it was generally agreed that the chain-mail had helped to save the ship and the lives of its men. On the other hand, they did have something to show off, the unexploded shell in the stern-post, and this became a much valued show-piece in the naval museum in Washington.

'Kearsage' had been hovering about the French coast for months, and was certainly due for a rest. When she appeared in New York, Winslow and his crew were greeted with flags, bunting and invitations from the grateful citizens, while the merchants of Boston got up a special banquet in their honour. The criticisms surrounding Winslow's actions were quickly forgotten. Instead, the heroes were at once surrounded by reward, flattering compliment and well-deserved applause, wherever they went. The sense of relief and achievement was intense. As Admiral Farragut said; "I would sooner have fought that fight than any on the ocean". They even got a poem in their honour:

> Hail to the 'Kearsage' - Bungay
>
> Hail to the 'Kearsage', castle of oak,
> And pride of the heaving sea !
> Hail to her guns, whose thunder awoke
> The waves, and startled with lightening stroke
> The nations that should be free !
> Hail to her captain and crew !
> Hail to her banner blue!
> Hail to her deathless name !
> Hail to her granite name !
>
> The British lion may cease his roar:
> For his darling privateer,
> At sea a pirate, a thief on shore,
> Now lies a wreck on the ocean floor,
> No longer a buccaneer.
> Hail to our Yankee tars !
> Hail to the stripes and stars !
> Hail Winslow, chief of the seas !
> Hail to his victory !
>
> Cheer ! 290 the robber is dead,
> And Semmes, the pirate in chief,
> A swordless coward, defeated, has fled,
> Bearing the curse of the sea on his head,
> To England, the home of the thief.
> Hail to our holy cause !
> Hail to our equal laws !
> Hail to the peace to be !
> Hail to all nations free !

So much did it mean to the North that 'Alabama' had gone. And what of the Confederate officers now in England ? For a time, indeed, they enjoyed themselves in the social life of London, but that didn't last – they had after all been defeated. Nor was the war going well at home. It was possible to stay and join the officer pool still in Europe, but with little opportunity available, that seemed a poor choice. Semmes and Kell both felt they could be better employed.

Semmes got back to the Confederacy by sailing to Mexico, crossing the border into Texas, then by being smuggled across the Mississippi. From there on he could take a train to Richmond, itself a remarkable journey in those days, and arrived there in January 1865. He took up a post as commander of the James River Fleet, covering Richmond, and held that until the end of the war.

Kell shipped on a blockade runner directly into one of the few ports open on the Confederate east coast. He, too, served on the James River, but was eventually invalided out.

Note 1.   Raphael Semmes' challenge to the captain of the 'Kearsage' (taken from 'Destruction of the American carrying trade' by F.M. Edge).

"To   A.D.Bonfils Esq   C.S.S. 'Alabama'
      Cherbourg
      !4th June 1864

   Sir,
   I hear that you were informed by the United States Consul that the 'Kearsage' was to come to this port solely for the prisoners landed by me, and that she was to depart in 24 hours. I desire you to say to the United States Consul that my intention is to fight the 'Kearsage' as soon as I can make the necessary arrangements. I hope these will not detain me later than until tomorrow evening, or after the morrow morning at farthest. I beg she will not depart before I am ready to go out.
         I have the honour to be
            Very respectfully, your obedient servant
               R.Semmes, Captain"

'Prize List' of C.S.S 'Alabama' 1862/3/4

Name	Home Port	From/To	Type	Cargo	Date Taken	Fate
'Ocmulgee'	Edgartown		Whaler		2nd Sept 1862	Burned
'Starlight'	Boston	Fayal/Boston	Schooner		7th Sept	Burned
'Ocean Rover'	Mass		Whaler	Oil	8th Sept	Burned
'Alert'	New London	India	Barque	Clothing	9th Sept	Burned
'Weather Gauge'	Provincetown		Schooner		9th Sept	Burned
'Altamaha'	New Bedford		Brig		13th Sept	Burned
'Benjamin Tucker'			Whaler	Oil	14th Sept	Burned
'Courser'	Provincetown		Whaler		16th Sept	Target
'Virginia'	New Bedford		Whaler		17th Sept	Burned
'Elisha Dunbar'	New Bedford		Whaler		18th Sept	Burned
'Emily Farnum'	New York	N Y/Liverpool		Grain	3rd Oct	Burned
'Brilliant'	New York	N Y/London		Grain	3rd Oct	Burned
'Wave Crest'	New York	N Y/Cardiff	Barque	Grain	7th Oct	Target
'Dunkirk'	New York	N Y/Lisbon	Brig	Grain	7th Oct	Burned
'Tonawanda'	Philadelphia	Philad/Liverpool	Ship	Grain	11th Oct	Bonded $80,000
'Manchester'	New York	N Y/Liverpool	Ship	Grain	11th Oct	Burned
'Lamplighter'	Boston	N Y/Gibralter	Barque	Tobacco	15th Oct	Burned
'Lafayette'	Boston	Boston/Belfast		Grain	23rd Oct	Burned
'Crenshaw'		N Y/Glasgow		Mixed	26th Oct	Burned
'Lauretta'	Boston	N Y/Madeira	Barque	Cotton	28th Oct	Burned
'Baron de Custine'		Bangor/Cardenas	Brig	Lumber	29th Oct	Bonded $6,000
'Levi Starbuck'	New Bedford		Whaler		2nd Nov	Burned
'C.B. Wales'	Boston	Calcutta/Boston	Schooner	Linseed	8th Nov	Burned
'Parker Cook'	Boston	Boston/Cayes	Barque	Prov.	30th Nov	Burned
'Nina'	Baltimore	Baltimore/Jamaica			5th Dec	Bonded $15,000
'Ariel'		N Y/Aspinwall		Mail	Dec	Bonded $261,000
'Golden Rule'	New York	N Y/Aspinwall			26th Jan 1863	Burned
'Chastelain'	Boston	Martinique/ Cienfuegos	Brig	Wood	31st Jan	Burned
'Palmetto'	New York	N Y/ Puerto Rico		Prov.	3rd Feb	Burned
'Olive Jane'	New York	Bordeaux/N Y		Wine	21st Feb	Burned
'Golden Eagle'	Howland's	Cork		Guano	21st Feb	Burned
'Washington'	New York	Chincha Is./Antwerp (Peru)		Guano	27th Feb	Bonded $50,000
'Bethia Thayer'		Rockland/Chincha Is. (Peru)		Guano	1st Mar	Bonded $50,000
'Punjaub'	Boston	Calcutta/London		Linseed	12th Mar	Bonded $55,000

Name	Home Port	From/To	Type	Cargo	Date Taken	Fate
'Morning Star'	Boston	Calcutta/London		Linseed	23rd Mar	Bonded
'Kingfisher'	Fairhaven		Whaler		23rd Mar	Burned
'Charles Hill'	Boston	Liverpool/Montevideo		Salt	24th Mar	Burned
'Nora'	Boston	Liverpool/Calcutta		Salt	24th Mar	Burned
'John A.Parks'	Maine	N Y/ Buenos Aires		Pine	28th Mar	Burned
'Louisa Hatch'				Coal	4th April	Burned
'Kate Cory'	Westport		Brig		14th April	Burned
'Lafayette'	New Bedford		Whaler	Oil	4th April	Burned
'Nye'	New Bedford		Whaler		1st May	Burned
'Dorcas Prince'		N Y/Shanghai		Coal	1st May	Burned
'Union Jack'	Boston		Barque		2nd May	Burned
'Sea Lark'	New York		Ship		2nd May	Burned
'Gildersliene'					25th May	Burned
'Justina'			Barque		25th May	Bonded
'Jabez Snow'	Rockport		Ship		26th May	Burned
'Amazonian'	Boston	N Y/Montevideo			2nd June	Burned
'Talisman'			Ship		June	Burned
'Conrad'		Philadelphia/B A		Wool	June	Converted New York
'Anna F.Schmidt'		Boston/San Francisco			2nd July	Burned
'Express'	Boston	Callao/Antwerp		Guano	4th July	Burned
'Sea Bride'			Barque	Wool	5th Aug	Sold
'Amanda'	Boston	Manilla/ Queenstown	Barque	Sugar	6th Nov	Burned
'Winged Racer'	New York	N Y/Manilla	Clipper	Jute	10th Nov	Burned
'Contest'	New York	Yokahama/N Y	Clipper	Luxuries	11th Nov	Burned
'Martaban'			Barque	Rice	24th Dec	Burned
'Sonora'	Mass.	Singapore/Akyab		Ballast	26th Dec	Burned
'Highlander'	Boston	Singapore/Akyab		Ballast	26th Dec	Burned
'Emma Jane'	Maine	Bombay/Amherst		Ballast	15th Jan 1864	Burned
'Rockingham'		Callao/Cork		Guano	22nd Apr	Target
'Tycoon'	New York	N Y/ San Francisco		Mixed.	27th Apr	Burned

Prize of C.S.S. 'Tuscaloosa'

'Santee'				Rice	31st July 1863	Bonded $150,000

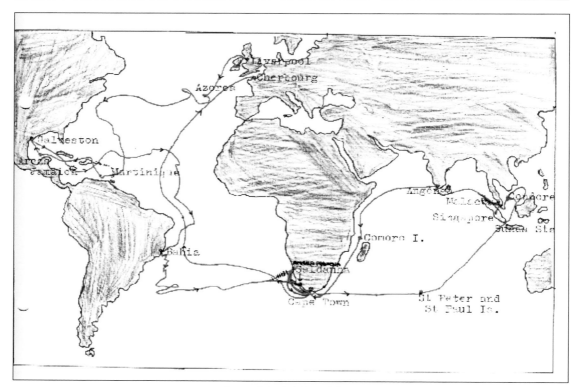

Cruise of the C.S.S. Alabama
August 1862 - June 1864

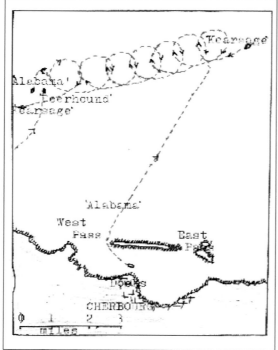

C.S.S. Alabama vs. U.S.S. Kearsage
June 19th, 1864

Final position of each ship, and of the
'Deerhound' shown

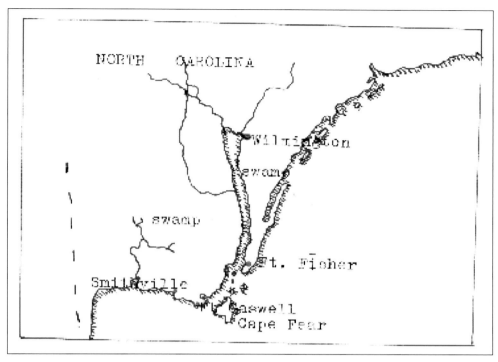

Wilmington, North Carolina

Chapter Twelve

Final cruise of the 'Florida'

During the events of Chapter 9 'Florida' was part of the Confederate concentration in France. When that broke up in early 1864, she had been taken out of Brest by her new captain Charles M. Morris. Her departure was certainly quicker than anticipated, but the intention was clear enough. She would try her luck again in the Atlantic Ocean, being fully repaired and with a fresh captain and crew. Perhaps even after 'Alabama', 'Georgia' and 'Florida' herself had taken their pick, there might still be a few enemy ships; if not, there was always the coastal gathering off New England and New York.

However, first call was to Madeira, where Morris had been informed he could find large stocks of coal – sufficient supply for many months. Perhaps a merchant vessel or two might also be discovered. But it was not to be. Indeed, as soon as Morris came into harbour, he was blockaded by the U.S.S. 'St. Louis', recently arrived from Spain. This was something of a surprise, for Morris had expected every available U.S. naval vessel to be converging upon Brest. As he was aware only of 'Kearsage', he assumed no others were anywhere near the European coast.

In Madeira, too, there was trouble with the coal supply. The government was Portuguese, and they took a rigorously neutral attitude. Minimal coal stocks would be released to 'Florida', and that only under considerable pressure. It was obvious that the locals felt embarrassment at the Confederate presence – in fact, Morris was asked to leave as soon as possible.

The old sloop 'St. Louis' couldn't really hope to stop 'Florida'. She had no steam power for one thing – probably why she was not part of the Brest blockade – and was not as well armed. 'Florida' would certainly have been able to sink her. But Morris was unwilling to risk damage to his own ship at this stage; he might find himself crippled without anywhere to go for repair. So he wisely decided on a quick escape, even though he had loaded only 20 tons of coal. It wasn't difficult. Staying close to land, he used the camouflaging effect of the hilly background to conceal his ship until the last moment, then made a dash for the sea, leaving 'St. Louis' far behind.

'Florida' cruised for some time in mid Atlantic, without much success. As had partly been expected, there were few United States vessels about: only one was seen and captured before their ocean crossing was complete. Next Morris visited St. Pierre, Martinique, where she was able to coal from ample French supplies. Where now ? His second choice was the coastal trade off America, so Bermuda had to be next call, where he could base himself for a protracted stay – if allowed. 'Florida' left Martinique on the 7th of May.

As seen in the last chapter, Bermuda became very difficult for the Confederate Navy in late 1864. However, in May and June that situation was still some way off. 'Florida' was received with approval. In all she remained based in Bermuda for three months, going out to attack American shipping between New York and Bermuda itself, and returning 'home' unopposed, to refuel. In June, for example, she was given five days permission for the harbour, stayed nine, and coaled 135 tons, six times as much as in Madeira. At least five merchant ships fell to 'Florida' during the period, mainly close to New York, although the fishing fleet was not attacked by her. Much destruction, panic and misery were inflicted in the name of the South. Truthfully, though, she couldn't have done it without the goodwill in Bermuda: and where were the enemy warships ?

In August 'Florida' cruised leisurely across the Atlantic to Tenerife, there to pick up supplies and fuel. Then Morris brought her back to the Brazilian coast, and on the 5th of October 1864, having captured another nine merchant ships, put into Bahia – a big mistake, as it turned out. 'Florida's presence nearby had already been proclaimed to the world, since Morris had been lingering outside the port for days. Inside, indeed, lay the U.S.S. 'Wachusett', commanded by Captain Napoleon Collins.

Morris was obviously relying on the international laws of neutrality. No belligerent would attack another in a third party's harbour. He felt perfectly secure, enough to allow him and most of the crew to step ashore.

He didn't know Collins. War changes men and rules sometimes get ignored. It was arranged that 'Wachusett' should slip her anchor – in error, of course – at a given time, and, as if by accident, would crash bow first into the unsuspecting Confederate. Collins would protest his horror at the occurrence later – but the 'Florida' would have sunk.

On the 7th of October, then, the 'Wachusett' moved out under minimum sail, gathering momentum past a Brazilian gunboat on guard, and rammed home under the 'Florida's starboard quarter, splintering bulwarks and mizzen to the deck. But the steersman had bungled, the 'Florida' did not sink, and as 'Wachusett' backed off, the few men actually still on board ran in a frightened way around the decks, looking for damage and grabbing weapons to repel any boarders. There were scarce enough to make any defence at all.

Napoleon Collins rather overplayed his hand at this point. Had he apologised to the Confederates and Brazilian authority, he might well have got away with his faulty anchor story. But the Union commander seemed to lose his head. He ordered rapid fire from the small guns at his bow, and called upon his men to force the cruiser's surrender.

There wasn't much opposition. Even the few available crewmen on 'Florida' lost their chance, as mast, sails and spars came thundering down to pin them to the deck. One officer, Lt. Stone, managed to free himself, and fired a shot from his pistol. But that was it. The cruise of the 'Florida' had ended in confusion and bad luck, with just a leavening of the ludicrous.

However, Morris and his men ashore were not amused. Rushing down to the beach, they met several dripping survivors, who had managed to swim away. Those pointed to the 'Florida', now moving toward the harbour entrance towed by 'Wachusett'. The Brazilian gunboats, which might have been expected to intervene, did nothing effective.

'Florida' was taken all the way up to Hampton Roads, to lie off Fort Monroe, Virginia, very much a Union stronghold. Immediately she was an attraction for visitors, for people who had heard so much about a commerce raider second only to 'Alabama' in reputation and success. Few had seen the 'Alabama', and that made 'Florida' even more glamorous. No-one outside the government blamed Collins for breaking international law, though his action had to be condemned ultimately, and he was dismissed the service. An apology found its way to Brazil..

'Florida' was sunk eventually, after yet another collision with an army transport. The United States government was taking no risks. Those of her crew captured with the ship were taken north, ironically being transferred to Captain Winslow's 'Kearsage' on her way home. The arrival in Boston for the victor over 'Alabama' was thus even more sweet, as he gave the news of 'Florida's demise.

As for Morris and the others stranded in Bahia, they faced a long trip to England, there to pass on more bad news to the European Confederates. The loss of 'Florida' was a grievous blow, not only to the striking power of the Confederate States Navy, but to morale throughout the service. 'Florida' had been a fine ship in her lifetime. She had carried the Confederate colours into many seas, and had acquitted herself brilliantly in pursuit of her purpose – 37 prizes taken in all. As with the 'Alabama', the mere existence of 'Florida' had an even greater effect on their mutual enemy than the number of sinkings recorded: and if her end seemed of less moment than 'Alabama's, that was a result of the war situation. In mid 1864 the Confederates still seemed to be able to hold things together, whereas by October they were plainly heading for defeat.

Prize List of C.S.S. 'Florida'

Name	Date Taken	Name	Date Taken
'Estelle'	20th January 1863	'F.B.Cutting'	6th August 1863
'Windward'	22nd January 1863	'Avon'	20th August 1863
'Corrisanne'	22nd January 1863	'General Berry'	1863
'Jacob Bell'	12th February 1863	'Southern Cross'	February 1864
'Star of Peace'	12th March 1863	'George Latimer'	18th May 1864
'Aldebaran'	12th March 1863	'Harriet Stevens'	1st July 1864
'Lapwing'	28th March 1863	'Golconda'	8th July 1864
'M.J.Colcord'	13th March 1863	'M.Y.Davis'	9th July 1864
'Commonwealth'	17th April 1863	'Electric Spark'	10th July 1864
'Henrietta'	23rd April 1863	'Anglo Saxon'	20th August 1864
'Oneida'	24th April 1863	'Mondamin'	26th July 1864
'Clarence'	6th May 1863	'Arabella'	Aug-Sept 1864
'Crown Point'	13th May 1863	'Greenland'	Aug-Sept 1864
'Red Gauntlet'	14th June 1863	'Windward'	Aug-Sept 1864
'B.F.Hoxie'	16th June 1863	'Southern Rights'	Aug-Sept 1864
'V.H.Hill'	27th June 1863	'W.C.Clark'	Aug-Sept 1864
'Sunrise'	7th July 1863	'Zelinda'	Aug-Sept 1864
'N.B.Nash'	8th July 1863	'David Lapsley'	Aug-Sept 1864
'Rienzi'	8th July 1863		

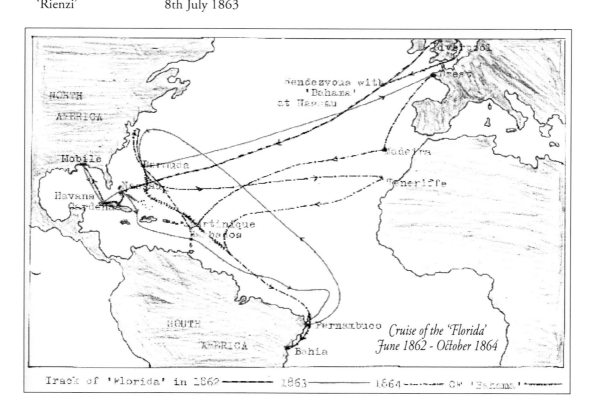

Cruise of the 'Florida'
June 1862 - October 1864

Track of 'Florida' in 1862 ------ 1863 ———— 1864 ---- Of 'Bahama'

an international crew – it was said no fewer than fourteen languages were spoken aboard – Waddell had gained their affection.

The sailors had indeed good reason to be satisfied, for the present, at least. A seaman's life was always hard, but the Confederates, whatever the progress of their war, were determined at any cost to preserve goodwill. More drink was distributed, more privileges granted, more pay provided than to any other naval or merchant ship afloat. It was certainly felt to be necessary. Such nationless men as sailors were, might easily switch their loyalty should temptation arise.

The Indian Ocean proved empty of United States merchantmen, rather a disappointment to Waddell, because one of those taken by the end of the year had been a whaler. If that was a straggler from the main fleet, then perhaps the others would not be far ahead: but it was not so. Melbourne was reached without further incident on the 25th of January 1865.

Here again began one of those struggles between a Confederate captain and the authorities over laws of neutrality. Strictly speaking, 'Shenandoah' should only have been allowed 48 hours in Melbourne before leaving port: and this might have happened. The United States consul was immediately busy trying to enforce that ruling. However, Waddell managed to find something wrong with his propeller shaft, and, by the laws, he was allowed to see to necessary repair. The 'Shenandoah' was ordered into dry dock, and a day by day examination begun. Waddell had other reasons, of course, for his delaying tactics. He wanted to recruit more sailors, because his ship was still undermanned. As usual the Confederate way was helped by its popularity among local people – the newspapers seemed to be on his side.

There was in fact some trouble. Clashes between seamen and American immigrants in Melbourne took place, and the 'Shenandoah' had to be protected by Australian police. On at least one occasion legal objections were raised about men being enlisted. Pressure on Waddell mounted, and there were signs that their popularity was waning. It was time to leave.

'Shenandoah' floated off again on the 17th of February, after coaling 300 tons, and was on her way next day – with 42 extra men, mostly British subjects. The last Confederate cruiser disappeared into the Pacific Ocean.

For six months there was no news of 'Shenandoah'. Their war had ended by then. Indeed, there was no one left to care about her. Then on the 20th of July the whaler 'Nile' put into San Francisco, overloaded with survivors from the many sinkings 'Shenandoah' had apparently made. The news was electrifying. Somewhere in the North Pacific a Confederate cruiser was still waging war, presumably in ignorance.

Waddell's course after leaving Melbourne had taken him north, searching now for the elusive whaling fleet. Months passed without a sighting, and then on the 1st of April the tall masts of American whalers were finally observed – four of them, clustered near the tropical Mariana Islands: and so it began. The whalers were scattered all the way to the north, generally out of sight of each other. It was easy work for 'Shenandoah', except for the accumulation of prisoners, as one after another the whalers were burned. Eventually two of them, the 'James Maury' and the 'Milo' had to be bonded to carry hundreds of men home. In a great climax on 28th June, ten ships were taken and burned, while an eleventh, the 'Nile' was bonded – it was she who brought the news to San Francisco.

'Shenandoah' had now destroyed a substantial part of the whaling fleet, 29 in all, out of a total of 38 for the whole cruise. The cruiser had also reached the Bering Straits, their target area by the plan. Waddell sailed north only until he encountered pack ice, then turned south-east to parallel the American coast.

However, he was now a worried man. Some of the recent prisoners had expressed their belief that the war was over. They had heard somewhere, vaguely, that hostilities had ceased weeks ago, perhaps even at the end of April. Waddell discredited rumours, but he became uneasy. It simply wasn't safe or fair to continue the action under these conditions. Balancing that thought, many of the prisoners had enlisted from whalers taken on the 28th – had effectively signed on in the service of the Confederate States. Who was right ? It was sensible to continue the cruise, but to keep to recognised trade routes in the hope of receiving definite news.

On and on they sailed, through July and into August, until they came across a British barque, the H.M.S. 'Barracouta'. Ominously it hove to, waiting for 'Shenandoah', and the news carried in a message from James Bulloch was bad. The war was over, had been since the last surrender on the 3rd of June; the Confederate States were no longer in existence. It was a bitter blow for Waddell. Here he was, effectively a pirate, for most of his destructive work had been after the 3rd of June. His 'stars and bars' at the masthead meant nothing – any vessel of any nation was entitled to attack and destroy a pirate ship. Nor would he be able to enter any port for protection.

Waddell decided to consult his men. Their decision must be his, for they faced the same trouble as he. The men were naturally divided. Some wanted to run for the nearest non-American port, arguing that they were safer in the hands of a neutral. Some chose Australia, inevitably, the men who had joined there. Some wanted to head for Britain, some Cape Town, but none, of course, selected the United States. The final decision was for Waddell, as it was always going to be: and Waddell went for Britain, specifically Liverpool, to be reached by sailing far from land, avoiding all contact with other people. At least, Waddell thought, there was a chance of some sympathy in that city.

Down came the Confederate ensign. All fires were doused – there must be no smoke – and gun ports closed, the guns themselves rapidly dismounted. No one must be able to accuse them of being a ship of war. Then once again 'Shenandoah' disappeared from the world, her only notice being from the 'Barracouta' encounter. Her route followed the coast of America right down to Cape Horn, past that, and north again to cut across first the South, then the North Atlantic. In other words 'Shenandoah' went right around the world.

Waddell had in doing so conducted a marvellous piece of navigation, for not until November did he see land again. It was a perfect landfall, too, right outside the Mersey estuary. On the 6th of November 1865 'Shenandoah' sailed up into the river, to drop anchor off Liverpool. She carried aloft the 'stars and bars' for the last time – the last Confederate – to be a spectacle for the curious.

After the formalities of a low-key welcome, 'Shenandoah' was offered for sale, and continued her career as a merchant vessel, the 'Majidi', carrying goods for the Sultan of Zanzibar. She was finally sunk in 1879.

Those members of the crew, whose British citizenship made them liable to prosecution, took American nationality, and were allowed to go their own way. The other crewmen had no problems even of that kind. James Waddell and his officers were eventually pardoned for their actions, and went home – Waddell himself continued on the sea until 1877, as a captain on the San Francisco mailboats, then retired to live quietly in Annapolis. Waddell died in 1886 at the age of 62.

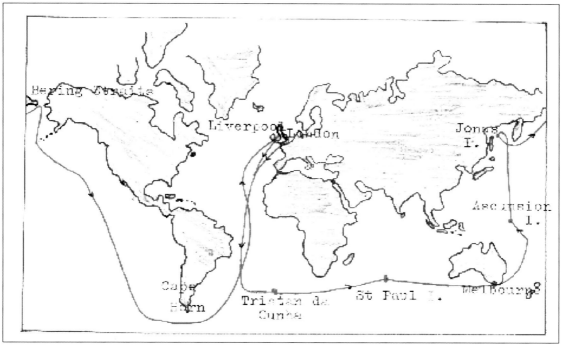

Cruise of the 'Shenandoah'; October 1864 - November 1865

Prize List of C.S.S. 'Shenandoah'

Name	Type	Date of Capture	Fate
'Alina'	Barque	29th October 1864	Burned
'Charter Oak'	Schooner	5th November 1864	Burned
'D.Godfrey'	Barque	7th November 1864	Burned
'Susan'	Brig	10th November 1864	Burned
'Kate Prince'	Ship	12th November 1864	Bonded
'Adelaide'	Barque	12th November 1864	Bonded
'Lizzie M. Stacey'	Schooner	13th November 1864	Burned
'Edward'	Whaler	4th December 1864	Burned
'Delphine'	Barque	29th December 1864	Burned
'Edward Casey'	Whaler	1st April 1865	Burned
'Harvest'	Whaler	1st April 1865	Burned
'Hector'	Whaler	1st April 1865	Burned
'Pearl'	Whaler	1st April 1865	Burned
'Euphrates'	Whaler	21st June 1865	Burned
'Abigail'	Whaler	21st June 1865	Burned
'Wm. Thompson'	Whaler	21st June 1865	Burned
'Jireh Swift'	Whaler	22nd June 1865	Burned
'James Maury'	Whaler	22nd June 1865	Bonded
'Susan Abigail'	Trader	23rd June 1865	Burned
'Sophia Thornton'	Whaler	25th June 1865	Burned
'Nimrod'	Whaler	26th June 1865	Burned
'Isabelle'	Whaler	26th June 1865	Burned
'General Pilse'	Whaler	26th June 1865	Burned
'Catherine'	Whaler	26th June 1865	Burned
'Gipsy'	Whaler	26th June 1865	Burned
'Milo'	Whaler	26th June 1865	Bonded
'W.C.Nye'	Whaler	26th June 1865	Burned
'Waverley'	Whaler	28th June 1865	Burned
'Favorite'	Whaler	28th June 1865	Burned
'Nile'	Whaler	28th June 1865	Bonded
'Isaac Howland'	Whaler	28th June 1865	Burned
'Congress'	Whaler	28th June 1865	Burned
'Martha'	Whaler	28th June 1865	Burned
'Hillman'	Whaler	28th June 1865	Burned
'Brunswick'	Whaler	28th June 1865	Burned
'Nassau'	Whaler	28th June 1865	Burned
'Covington'	Whaler	28th June 1865	Burned
'Fillmore'	Whaler	28th June 1865	Burned

The Achievement

To summarise: Confederate naval policy from 1861 to 1865 was based on the need to keep Southern ports open. The Confederacy had much less manufacturing capability than the United States, and it was realised from the start of the war that most necessary manufactures would have to be imported. It was also necessary for cotton, their biggest crop, to be exported to pay for those imports.

For their ports to be kept open the Confederates would have to prevent a blockade, or if that occurred, would have to take retaliatory action. But the South had few ships, certainly not enough to offer open battle to the United States Navy. When a blockade was established almost straight away in 1861, there was little which could be done immediately to break it. So the South turned to other ideas which had some chance of either destroying the blockading ships or of finding a way around them.

From the land came submarines, mines and torpedo boats, all ingenious new inventions of the Civil War, which sank a few Yankee ships, but which only saw their real development in later years. Ironclads, which were wooden ships with steel sheets about them, designed to withstand the new explosive shells being supplied, had their day. The battle between two of them in 1862, the U.S.S. 'Monitor' and C.S.S. 'Merrimac', became famous as the first between iron ships. But they were still too primitive to make a decisive impression. They, too, developed within a few years sufficiently to take over from wooden vessels (the 'Stonewall' might have done, but was too late), but not before the end of the Civil War. The blockade remained intact under assault by all these innovations.

The creation of specially designed ships to run past warships guarding the ports was moderately successful, and for a few years profitable for their owners. However, the blockades were gradually tightened, and increasing numbers of blockade-runners were captured, until the volume of goods arriving in those ships was too small to make any difference. The effectiveness of the blockade is described in 'Naval History of the Civil

War', by Howard Nash, 1972: by the end of the war 1149 blockade-runners had been captured, of which 210 were steam powered. Another 335 vessels had been burned or driven ashore, of which 85 were steamers. All these amounted to a value of $31 million. In the opinion of Mr.Nash the North won because of the blockade.

Commerce raiding was probably the only way the Confederates could fight a naval war. The reasons why and the methods used have been described in this book: and taken in isolation the resulting campaign was successful. The United States merchant fleet was greatly reduced by sinkings or transfer to neutral flag. It did not recover for many years after the war. The assistance given to the Confederate campaign by neutral countries was significant – as a postscript to this work the post-war 'Alabama' Arbitration, in which Britain admitted responsibility for much of the raider damage, is described.

Another effect of the Confederate cruisers was to carry knowledge of the war out into the world. The appearance of these lone ships in the ports of Spain, England, France, the West Indies and South America encouraged some understanding of and sympathy for the Southern cause. For a time the Confederate States came quite close to being recognised in Europe, and in this process their successful operations on the sea certainly helped.

This was the last war in which sail took a leading part. The transition to steam had been under way even before then, of course, but was quickened by it. A high proportion of ships captured at sea were sailing ships, unable to outrun the power of steam. By the end of the 1870s sail had disappeared as a medium for transportation, passenger service and warships.

Commerce raiding itself did not disappear. After all the arguments about the legitimacy of this form of warfare – Confederate sailors were often described as pirates – it was realised that destruction of supplies in shipment could have a decisive impact. Just consider the U-Boat activities in the two World Wars. The 'Alabama' example showed how efficient a raider system could be, in which huge amounts of damage could be caused by single vessels.

Here is a summary of achievements of the Confederate States Navy.

Table 1 – Confederate Cruisers and their Prizes

Name of ship	Length of career – including Months in port during cruise	Ships captured/burned/ bonded					
		1861	1862	1863	1864	1865	Total
'Nashville'	4 months	2	-	-	-	-	2
'Sumter'	7 months	16	2	-	-	-	18
'Florida'	26 months	-	-	22	15	-	37
'Clarence/ 'Tacony'/ Archer'	2 months	-	-	21	-	-	21
'Alabama'	22 months	-	26	35	3	-	64
'Tuscaloosa'	6 months	-	-	1	-	-	1
'Georgia'	14 months	-	-	9	-	-	9
'Tallahassee'	3 months	-	-	-	30	-	30
'Olustee'	2 weeks	-	-	-	6	-	6
'Chickamauga'	2 weeks	-	-	-	7	-	7
'Shenandoah'	14 months	-	-	-	9	29	38
All Privateers	various	47	-	-	-	-	47
Total		65	28	88	70	29	280

Table 2 – Location of Prizes

	1861	1862	1863	1864	1865	Total
Off United States/Confederate Coast	48	4	27	48	-	127
Off Brazilian Coast	2	-	31	17	-	50
In Atlantic Ocea	7	22	10	2	-	41
In Caribbean/Gulf of Mexico	8	2	12	-	-	22
In Indian Ocean	-	-	8	3	-	11
In Pacific Ocean	-	-	-	-	29	29
Total	65	28	88	70	29	280

The 'Alabama' arbitration

Information mainly taken from Encyclopaedia Britannica, 1957 edition.

Following their Civil War the United States government took legal action against Great Britain. They had two grievances: first, the recognition of the Southern States as belligerents and a general manifestation of unfriendliness in other ways; second, the breach of neutrality in allowing the 'Alabama', the 'Florida', the 'Shenandoah' and other Confederate vessels to be built and equipped on British territory. Those ships had caused much trouble and had cost the United States a great deal of money. Recompense was therefore sought by them, to be known thereafter as the 'Alabama' claims.

Correspondence between the countries extended over several years, but in 1871 a commission was appointed by them to determine how the matters should be settled. Eventually three rules were agreed upon: a neutral government is bound (1) to use due diligence to prevent the fitting out, arming or equipping within its jurisdiction of any vessel, which it has reasonable grounds to believe is intended to cruise or carry on war against a power with which it is at peace, and also to prevent the departure from its jurisdiction of such a vessel, it having been specially adapted, in whole or in part, to warlike use; (2) not to permit either belligerent to make use of its ports or waters as the base of naval operations against the other, or for the augmentation of military supplies or men; (3) to use due diligence in its own ports and waters to prevent any violation of the obligations mentioned.

These three rules were embodied in the Treaty of Washington in 1871, which referred the 'Alabama' claims to a tribunal composed of five arbitrators, one to be named by each party, three to be neutral. The Tribunal had power to award a sum if Great Britain were found in the wrong.

After some delay caused by consideration of indirect losses – for instance, higher insurance payments, it was agreed that indirects be excluded.

The arbitrators were: for the United States Mr C.F.Adams, for Great Britain Sir Alexander Cockburn, and neutrals Count Sclopis (Italy), M.Staempfli (Switzerland) and Baron d'Itajuba (Brazil).

By September 1873 the tribunal had decided to accept the case of the United States. It found that Great Britain was legally responsible for all the depredations of the 'Alabama' and 'Florida', and for all those committed by the 'Shenandoah' after she left Melbourne.

In the case of the 'Alabama' the court was unanimous. In the case of the 'Florida' Sir A. Cockburn alone dissented; in the case of 'Shenandoah' both he and Baron d'Itajuba dissented. In the case of the other vessels, the judgement was in favour of Great Britain.

The tribunal decided to award the United States a sum of $15,500,000 (£3,299,166) as damages - Sir A. Cockburn again dissenting. This was paid by Great Britain, who placed their future relations with the United States above a natural dislike of the award.

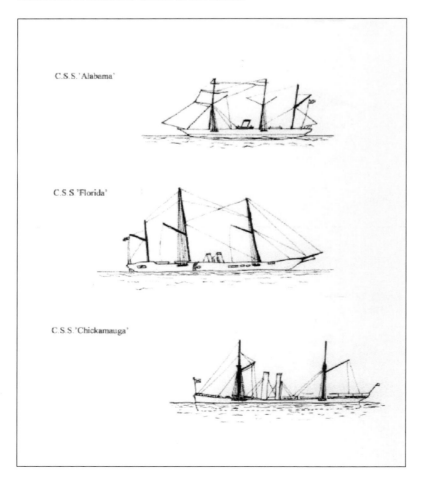

C.S.S. 'Alabama'

C.S.S 'Florida'

C.S.S. 'Chickamauga'

References

Sources used in each chapter are listed below

Chapters 1 and 2 –   'The American Civil War through British Eyes', volume 1,
                      November 1860 to April 1862; James and Patience Barnes, 2003.
                      'The Rebel Shore', James P. Merrill, 1957.
                      'The Navy in the Civil War – the Blockade and the Cruisers', Soley.
                      'History of American Privateers', Maclay.
                      'Confederate Privateers', W.H.Robinson.

Chapter 3 -   'History of the Confederate Navy', J.T.Scharff.
                     'My Adventures Afloat', Raphael Semmes.
                     'The American Civil War through British Eyes', as above.
                     'Service on Sumter and Alabama', R.Semmes, 1869.

Chapter 4   'The American Civil War through British Eyes', as above.
                     'Charles Francis Adams', L.F.Adams.
                     'Neutrality of Great Britain during the American Civil War', Bernard.
                     'Secret Service of the Confederate States in Europe', J.D Bulloch, 1883
                     'Europe and the American Civil War', Jordan and Platt.
                     'Number 290', S.Styles 1966.
                     'How the Confederate cruisers were equipped', J.D.Bulloch, 1883.

Chapter 5   'The Civil War Years', Robert E.Denney 1992.
                     'Sea Dogs of the Sixties', J.D.Hill.
                     'Atlantic Ocean', Rogers.
                     'Two Years on the Alabama', Sinclair.
                     'Career of the Alabama', W.E.Bennett,1964.
                     'The Florida', F.L.Owsley, 1965.

Chapter 6   'Prodigious Caribbean', Forbes.
                     'Two Years on the Alabama', Sinclair.

'The Civil War Years', Denney 1992.

Chapter 7   'Union and Confederate Navies', Soley.
'Atlantic Ocean', Rogers.
'Two Years on the Alabama', Sinclair.
'Story of the American Merchant Marine', Spears.
'American Merchant Marine', Marvin.

Chapter 8   'Two years on the Alabama', Sinclair.
'Indian Ocean', Rogers.

Chapter 9   'France and the Confederate Navy', Bigelow.
'Secret Service of the Confederate States in Europe', Bulloch.

Chapter 10   'Two Years on the Alabama', Sinclair.
'John Ancrum Winslow', Ellicott.
'The Alabama' Project', Appeal document, 1992.

Chapter 11   'The Rebel Shore', Merrill.

Chapter 12   'The Florida', F.L.Owsley, 1965.

Chapter 13   'The Yankee Whaler', Ashley.
'Rebel without a War', Robert F. Jones.

Chapter 14   'Britain's Maritime Heritage', Simper, 1982.

Postscript   'Encyclopaedia Britannica', 1957
'The Alabama Claims', A.Cook, 1975.
'Alabama and the Law', History Society of Lancashire and Cheshire, 1959.

Other Reading
'Introduction of the Ironclad Warship', Baxter.
'Rise and Fall of the Confederate Government', Davis.
'The Land they Fought for', Dowdey.
'Book of the Warship', Hawks.
'History of the US Navy', Knox.
'Paddle Wheel days in California', McMullen.
'History of the United States of America', Channing.
'History of the Civil War', Churchill.
'Encyclopaedia Britannica – American Civil War', 1957.
'Cotton Famine', M.Ellison, 1972.
'Ghost Ships of the Mersey', K.J. Williams.

Index

Note: 'inverted commas' indicate names of ships